WITHDRAWN

The Pioneer Woman Cooks

SUPER EASY!

The Pioneer Woman Cooks

SUPER EASY!

120 SHORTCUT RECIPES FOR DINNERS, DESSERTS, AND MORE

REE ✦ DRUMMOND

WM
WILLIAM MORROW
An Imprint of HarperCollinsPublishers

FIRST EDITION

Designed by Kris Tobiassen of Matchbook Digital

All food photography by Ed Anderson; page ii, v, viii (bottom), ix (left), ix (middle), xi (top), 16, 24, 32, 116, 140, 151, 168, 178, 210, 243, 258, 265, 268, 298, 315 by Ashley Alexander; viii (top) by Ladd Drummond; xiii, 106, 238 by Parker Chase; 36, 42, 186, 264 by Grant Daniels; 48, 102, 109 by Paige Drummond; 132 by Debbie Formby; 234 by Michael Dambrosia; 236 by Buff Strickland; all other photographs courtesy of Ree Drummond.

Library of Congress Cataloging-in-Publication Data has been applied for.

ISBN 978-0-06-296276-8

21 22 23 24 25 LSC 10 9 8 7 6 5 4 3 2 1

To Ladd

My super-cute partner in marriage, parenting, action movies, and life.
Thank you for being steadfast and sure. (Oh, and sexy!) ☺

Contents

INTRODUCTION

My first cookbook!

The kids were tiny.

This was twelve years ago!

We couldn't resist re-creating this cover!

I wrote my first cookbook in 2009, when I was just barely out of my thirties and the kids were all tiny. Our lives revolved around the ranch, where we homeschooled and the kids helped Ladd work cattle. I cooked for my family and the cowboys, and I blogged about all of our sweet rural experiences. Because the kids were small, there wasn't a whole lot that took us away from home. When Ladd snapped the photo that I used on that cookbook, I think I honestly believed things would always stay that way.

Well, as is always the case, things didn't stay that way! My kids got older and taller, and one by one, they've been leaving the nest for college and beyond. As the saying goes, the days were long but the years were short, and they seem to be getting shorter (as do I, comparatively speaking!). And of course, my cooking life has changed alongside everything else. What used to be a nice, predictable routine of breakfast, lunch, and dinner with little kiddos underfoot has morphed into a whole different one with a new set of rules.

Before I lay that out for you, let me give you a quick family update!

The Kids (and Family) Grew!

Alex, my oldest, just got married this year. She's all grown up and lives in Dallas with her new husband, Mauricio, and after working for a consulting firm right out of college, she now works for . . . her mom! Turns out my daughter has paid attention to my business goings-on through the years, and it's darn wonderful to have her on my team (in more ways than one).

FAVORITE RECIPE IN THIS BOOK:
Sheet Pan Mac and Cheese (page 184)

Paige is just starting her senior year in college, though it feels to me like she's been thirty years old for about a decade. Paige studies Hospitality Management and keeps me on my toes in many wonderful ways. I can't wait for her to be president someday! (Or whatever she wants to be.) I just hope she stays close to me!

FAVORITE RECIPE IN THIS BOOK:
Speedy Dumpling Soup (page 115)

Bryce started college a semester early last January so he could start playing spring ball with his football team, the University of North Texas Eagles. Being able to play D1 football in college was a longtime dream of Bryce's, and even though I hope he comes back to the ranch someday, it makes me happy to see him livin' the dream. Go, Bryce and Mean Green!

FAVORITE RECIPE IN THIS BOOK:
Classic Stromboli (page 147)

As for Todd? Well, he is no longer tiny. On the contrary, he's actually taller than Alex, Paige, and Bryce—which is fun, because he's the youngest in the family and it's nice for him to get the last word sometimes. Todd just started his junior year in high school and took his brother's place as quarterback of the Pawhuska Huskies! He's the funniest kid I know, and is still as sweet and kind as he was in that very first cookbook photo. (Again . . . just a little taller.)

FAVORITE RECIPE IN THIS BOOK:
Chicken-Fried Steak Fingers (page 205)

Oh hey, Jamar! Jamar is technically our foster son, but he's been a member of our family for over two years. He's one of the Drummond sibs at this point, and just started his freshman year in college. Jamar's playing football, too, and since our family loves football, Ladd and I are so excited to have three different games we can go watch on any given weekend. I miss this guy since he started college! (He loves food, as you can see from the lovestruck look on his face.)

FAVORITE RECIPE IN THIS BOOK:
Buffalo Chicken Totchos (page 53)

Mauricio!! He's my absolute favorite son-in-law and we all just love him. Because he came home a lot with Alex during quarantine, he became part of my TV crew, and he's always game to work, to help, and to eat! Mauricio and Alex are enjoying the newlywed life in Dallas, but they are able to come to the ranch a lot. Best of both worlds! Mauricio is definitely one of the good guys.

FAVORITE RECIPE IN THIS BOOK:
Festive Pork Chops (page 288)

Why Take the Easy Road?

So why *Super Easy*? Why now? Well, if you have a few moments, I'll tell ya!

1. LIFE IS CRAZY.

"I'm fine, everything's fine!"

The world has been (and is) crazy no matter who you are or where you live. This has trickled down to every area of life, and it was about April 2020—a mere month after everyone came home to quarantine—when I became very disenchanted with cooking in general. Wait a minute . . . I take that back. I didn't become disenchanted with cooking; I just got so tired of the daily grind. When everyone was home for those months, cooking wasn't fun like it had been when the kids were little and every day followed the same general schedule. It became drudgery, especially given the fact that all the kids were grown and tall and big and huge and would devour (within seconds) anything I cooked, whether I spent four hours or fourteen minutes making it.

2. "EASY" IS CONVENIENT.

Coconut Cream Pie
(page 325)

After hovering on the edge of exasperation, I started giving myself permission to chill out. To use more frozen bread dough as pizza crust. To switch to frozen mixed veggies for casseroles rather than finely dice them myself. To save the step of cooking rice and opt for the microwave version instead. And okay . . . to use jarred pesto with absolutely no guilt. To slap Cool Whip on top of the pie. To boldly go where I occasionally, but not regularly, had gone before. And here's the thing: once I crossed over that threshold and stopped trying to make everything I could from scratch, I fell in love with the peaceful, easy feeling that took over my cooking life. Now, don't get me wrong: I'd still say the majority of my meals are made with good from-scratch ingredients. I just work in way more easy substitutes now than I have in the past. And I like it.

But I didn't just sub in shortcuts; I also started gearing my recipes to require fewer steps. I opted for simplified processes, which translated to quick skillet meals, super-fast pastas, and casseroles that I'd mix and assemble right in the baking dish rather than in separate bowls and pans. "Easy" not only meant shortcut ingredients, it also meant simpler cooking. (Note: Deliciousness wasn't compromised at all!)

3. "EASY" IS FUN!

A couple of months after I had this easy cooking revelation, my kids started helping me film my Food Network show since my regular TV crew (they're from the UK) couldn't make the trip. We started demonstrating some of the glorious (and ridiculously simple) recipes I was whipping up as part of my new "easy game," and they became a regular part of the show. Rather than hear the outcry or uproar I was halfway expecting—after all, I'd started singing the praises of cake mix desserts and ten-minute soups—we had a great response from folks who watched the show. Turns out, everyone was looking for the lifeline that easy, breezy recipes can mean.

4. "EASY" IS ON TREND.

I'm sure waves of cooking trends come and go and perhaps before long we'll be back to all-day simmering soups and meals that take two or three hours to finish. But over the past year or two, I've noticed a real bent toward these kinds of "from scratch . . . sorta" recipes. I'm not sure if it's the influence of new social media worlds like TikTok or a younger generation having fun with super-simple (and photogenic) recipes—or maybe it's that we humans are just a little tired and need to give ourselves a break. It just seems that the days of food snobbery are starting to wane a bit. So be trendy! Cook all the recipes in this book!

5. "EASY" MEANS MORE TIME ENJOYING LIFE!

If there's one thing the last couple of years have shown us, it's that when it comes down to it, what really matters is the health and happiness of our loved ones—and having the time to relax, have fun, and enjoy life. Cooking, for me, has always been about bringing loved ones together around the table, and the simpler I can keep the meal itself, the more time and energy I have for Monopoly marathons, long walks with the dogs, or going on drives with Ladd (still my favorite thing in the world). More than ever, I cling to all the fun family moments!

Of course there's always a place for intricate, more complicated recipes when the occasion warrants—or when it feeds your creativity! I continue to be inspired by amazing chefs and food voices who go that extra mile and show us how beautiful food can be.

But for those times when you're looking for a simpler, easier approach for your everyday cooking (and eating), I hope you enjoy this super-fun cookbook . . . and the super-easy recipes within these pages.

Lots of love,

Ree

xoxo

I like shortCUTS and
I can not lie . . .

SUPERHERO SHORTCUTS

Think of these ingredients as the warp-speed button on your favorite recipes—and feel absolutely no guilt when you use them! They can shave lots of time off your cooking and baking, and that means more time hanging with your family, gardening, reading, or taking selfies with your dogs. (You all do that, right?)

BAGGED GREENS

BALSAMIC GLAZE

CAKE MIX

BAGGED SLAW

BOTTLED SALAD DRESSINGS

CANNED BEANS

BAKING MIX

BREADCRUMBS

CANNED GREEN CHILES

CANNED/PACKAGED SALMON

FROZEN BREAD DOUGH

FROZEN GREEN BEANS

CORNFLAKE CRUMBS

FROZEN DUMPLINGS

FROZEN PASTRY DOUGH

CREAMY CONDENSED SOUPS

FROZEN FISH STICKS

FROZEN POUND CAKE

DESSERT SAUCES

FROZEN FRUIT

FROZEN SHRIMP

FROZEN STUFFED PASTA

JARRED MARINARA

MULTIGRAIN PANCAKE MIX

INSTANT PUDDING

Life-changing!

MICROWAVE RICE AND GRAINS

NONDAIRY WHIPPED TOPPING

Jarred pesto is the best!

PACKAGED GNOCCHI

PREPARED MEATBALLS

QUICK RAMEN PACKETS

PREPARED BUTTERNUT SQUASH

MVP!
PREPARED PESTO

ROASTED CORN

PREPARED HUMMUS

PREPARED PIZZA DOUGH

SPICE BLENDS

MORE SUPERHEROES

Here are some more shortcut ingredients worth a big honorable mention! (I have all of these in my kitchen right now.) Canned/jarred artichoke hearts, wonton wrappers, canned pie filling (blueberry, apple, and cherry are my favorites), frozen biscuits, frozen diced onions, beef/chicken base, pre-hard-boiled eggs, canned enchilada sauce, no-cook lasagna noodles, and of course, canned whipped cream (woo-hoo!).

TOP NINE MUST-HAVE COOKING STAPLES

For flavor, for convenience, and for everyday cooking, I can't live without these everyday go-to ingredients . . . and you shouldn't either!

ASIAN-FLAVORED SAUCES

FRUIT JAMS AND JELLIES

JARRED AND CANNED PEPPERS

BOXED STOCKS AND BROTHS

GOOD BREAD

MUSTARDS

DRIED PASTA!

HOT SAUCES

TOMATO PRODUCTS

SHREDDED CHICKEN DIY

There are several recipes in this book that call for shredded cooked chicken. If you already have the chicken cooked, shredded, and ready to go, it can turn an otherwise time-consuming casserole, soup, or other recipe into a much, much faster proposition! Here are a few different approaches for quick shredded chicken.

Rotisserie Chicken

Let the deli do all the cooking! It doesn't get any easier than picking up a rotisserie chicken (or two) and shredding the meat when you get home. One rotisserie chicken will yield 4 to 4½ cups of shredded chicken, with a mix of white and dark meat.

1. Remove the rotisserie chicken from the package and use your hands (and/or two forks) to pull the meat apart into shreds. Discard the skin if you wish, but I like to get some of the skin in with the meat for flavor!

2. I like to divide the shredded chicken into 2-cup parcels so I have flexibility with the various recipes. Simply place the meat into 1-quart storage bags and roll them as you force out as much air as possible before sealing. Store them in the fridge for up to 4 days, or in the freezer for up to 6 months.

Cooking and Shredding Chicken

While the convenience of a rotisserie chicken can't be rivaled, there are other ways to ensure you're never, ever without all the shredded chicken you need to live a happy, stress-free life. The chicken part of your life, anyway!

If you prefer to cook and shred your own chicken rather than buy rotisserie, chicken breasts are the easiest way to go. You can buy large value packs of boneless, skinless breasts, cook them all at once, then shred and store the meat in the freezer. Here are different ways you can cook the chicken breasts. Each of the following methods cooks about 3 pounds of chicken breasts, to yield 4 to 4½ cups shredded chicken.

Same as with the rotisserie version, store the packaged chicken in the fridge for up to 4 days, or in the freezer for up to 6 months!

STOVETOP

Boiling chicken doesn't add any color to the meat, but it's great for casseroles and other settings where that doesn't matter! (It's super moist, too.)

1. Place chicken breasts in a pot of water (the water should cover the chicken by about 3 inches). Sprinkle in salt and pepper, then boil until fully cooked, 15 to 17 minutes.

2. Remove the chicken and set aside to cool until it can be handled.

3. Shred the boiled chicken with your hands or two forks or in a stand mixer using the paddle attachment.

OVEN

Roasting introduces a little more color and flavor to the chicken for things like tacos or sandwiches.

1. Preheat the oven to 425°F. Place the chicken breasts on a sheet pan, drizzle with olive oil, and sprinkle with salt and pepper.

2. Roast until cooked through, 22 to 24 minutes. Set aside to cool until it can be handled.

3. Shred as directed above for boiled chicken.

SLOW COOKER

Great to do when you have time to walk away and ignore it!

1. Place chicken breasts in a slow cooker.

3. Sprinkle in salt and pepper.

5. Shred the chicken right in the slow cooker using 2 forks, then drain off the liquid. (You can save the broth if you'd like!)

2. Add 1 cup chicken broth per 3 pounds of chicken.

4. Cover and cook on high for 3 to 4 hours or low for 7 to 8 hours.

INSTANT POT

Cooks the chicken in minutes . . . about 10 of them!

1. Place chicken breasts in an Instant Pot, sprinkle with salt and pepper, and add 1 cup chicken broth per 3 pounds of chicken.

2. Secure the lid and set the pressure valve to Sealing. Pressure cook the chicken for 10 minutes. Let the pressure release naturally for 5 minutes, then manually release the rest of the pressure.

3. Shred directly in the pot as with the slow cooker method.

My oldest and my youngest!

BREAKFAST

Bring back breakfast! (Just don't work too hard at it. ☺) In this crazy-busy world with our crazy-packed lives, it's easy to let breakfast disappear into the fast-food abyss—or, worse, to skip it altogether! Call me old-fashioned, but I like to think breakfast never went out of style, and to practice what I preach, I've put together a batch of recipes that are easy to make, scrumptious to eat, and take just a small sliver of time out of your morning. Some are sweet, some are savory, and all are totally delicious!

Made with boxed baking mix!

Chocolate Chip Scones

MAKES 8 SERVINGS

These sweet, delightful breakfast pastries would never pass for scones in the following geographic locations: the United Kingdom. But everywhere else on the globe, you're good! A measure of the tastiness of these scones is how irresistible they are to Todd, who usually declines scones on the basis that they aren't sweet enough. The kid could subsist on chocolate cake and Twinkies for the rest of his life, so trust me: If Todd devours these babies, the greatest sweet tooths in the world will, too.

SCONES

2½ cups baking mix (such as Bisquick), plus more for dusting

¼ cup packed brown sugar

4 tablespoons (½ stick) cold salted butter, cut into small pieces

2 large eggs, whisked

¼ cup buttermilk (or combine almost ¼ cup regular milk with a splash of white vinegar)

Splash of vanilla extract

1½ cups chocolate chips

ICING

3 cups sifted powdered sugar

¼ cup whole milk

Splash of vanilla extract

Pinch of kosher salt

¼ cup mini chocolate chips

1. Preheat the oven to 400°F. Line a baking sheet with parchment paper.

2. Make the scones: In a large bowl, mix the baking mix and brown sugar.

4. Add the eggs, buttermilk, and vanilla . . .

3. Add the butter and use a pastry blender or two knives to cut it into the dry ingredients until the mixture resembles coarse crumbs.

5. And stir until combined.

6. Add the chocolate chips and mix until everything comes together. Note: The dough will be very sticky!

7. Dust a work surface with some baking mix, turn the dough out onto it, and use your hands to form it into a ¾-inch-thick rectangle. Use a bench scraper or spatula to cut it into four equal portions.

8. Cut each portion in half diagonally (sprinkle baking mix on top if things get too sticky!) . . .

9. And carefully transfer the triangles to the lined baking sheet.

10. Bake until lightly browned, about 18 minutes. Set them aside to cool completely. (Try not to eat one yet!)

11. Make the icing: In a medium bowl, combine the powdered sugar, milk, vanilla, and salt . . .

12. And whisk until smooth and thick.

13. Use a spoon to drizzle the glaze over the scones in thick lines . . .

14. Then sprinkle on plenty of mini chocolate chips! Store at room temperature.

· ·

VARIATIONS

» *Instead of chocolate chips inside and on top, use chopped walnuts or pecans.*

» *For birthday scones, use rainbow sprinkles in the scones and on top of the glaze.*

» *Use a biscuit cutter to make round scones instead.*

Pineapple Smoothie Bowls

MAKES 2 TO 4 SERVINGS

Pretty, colorful smoothie bowls are all the rage, and this one uses a thick, delicious pineapple smoothie base that resembles Dole Whip, the famous frozen treat served at Disney World. Use your creativity to top the bowls with all the fruity colors of nature. The canvas is yours!

2 cups frozen pineapple chunks

1 cup vanilla yogurt

2 tablespoons sweetened condensed milk

½ to ¾ cup whole milk

⅓ cup blueberries

2 large strawberries, hulled and chopped

1 kiwi, peeled and thinly sliced

2 teaspoons chia seeds

¼ cup store-bought toasted coconut (sold in the snack section)

1. In a blender, combine the pineapple, yogurt, condensed milk, and ½ cup regular milk.

3. If it is very stubborn, add up to ¼ cup more milk to help it along.

5. And smooth the surface.

2. Blend until very smooth, scraping the sides of the blender as needed to help the mixture blend completely.

4. Pour the thick, yummy smoothie into a large shallow bowl . . .

6. Lay on the fruit in neat rows . . .

7. Then make a row of chia seeds . . .

8. And one of toasted coconut.

Happy breakfast! (Or snack. Or lunch. Or midnight feast!) This can be enjoyed as an epic single serving, or you can scoop out individual portions! (Or if you're feeling artsy, you can build individual bowls with the ingredients.)

VARIATIONS

» *Substitute sunflower seeds or pepitas for the chia seeds.*
» *Layer the pineapple smoothie and fruit in tall glasses for parfaits instead!*

SENSATIONAL SMOOTHIE BOWL IDEAS!

Blend your own amounts of these combos to reach the consistency you like! Smoothie bowls invite creativity. (These are more dessert-like than breakfast-like!)

Tropical: Blend frozen mango, frozen pineapple, yogurt, milk, and pineapple juice. Pour in a bowl and top with fresh or canned pineapple chunks, toasted coconut, sliced star fruit, and chia seeds. Drizzle with honey or agave syrup.

Strawberries and Cream: Blend frozen strawberries, yogurt, milk, sweetened condensed milk, and a little vanilla syrup. Pour in a bowl and top with sliced fresh strawberries, toasted sliced almonds, granola, and mini white chocolate chips. Drizzle with a little sweetened vanilla yogurt.

Chocolate Peanut Butter Banana: Blend frozen bananas with yogurt, milk, peanut butter, and chocolate chips. Pour in a bowl and top with rice cereal, sliced bananas, mini chocolate chips, and a drizzle of warm peanut butter.

Mixed Berry: Blend frozen mixed berries with yogurt, milk, pomegranate juice to get a deep pink color, and honey for sweetness. Pour in a bowl and top with granola, fresh blueberries, fresh raspberries, fresh blackberries, toasted coconut, and a small drizzle of chocolate sauce.

Protein: Blend frozen blackberries, fresh or frozen strawberries, yogurt, milk, peanut butter, walnuts, and a little vanilla syrup. Pour in a bowl and top with chopped walnuts, pepitas, and sliced almonds.

Raspberry Lemon: Blend frozen raspberries with yogurt, milk, and lemon zest. Pour in a bowl and top with toasted coconut, lemon zest, fresh raspberries, and sliced almonds. Drizzle with a little sweetened vanilla yogurt.

Other add-ins/toppers: coconut milk, pecans, kiwi, peach slices, apple slices, flaxseed, Grape-Nuts, cornflakes, cooked/cooled quinoa, chopped dried apricots, dried apples, dried bananas.

That's Dole Whip
underneath!

Bread Omelet

MAKES 1 SANDWICH (LARGE ENOUGH TO SERVE 2)

This recipe, which is really more about the method, went viral on social media in the past couple of years, and once I finally gave in and tried it, I discovered that it totally lived up to the hype. This amazing inside-out egg sandwich is as fun to make as it is yummy, and you won't be sorry for giving it a try.

5 large eggs, whisked

2 tablespoons milk

Kosher salt and black pepper

3 tablespoons salted butter

1 tablespoon canned chopped green chiles

1 tablespoon jarred pimientos

2 slices thick white bread (such as Texas toast)

2 slices pepper Jack cheese

Ketchup or spicy mustard, for serving

1. In a pitcher or spouted cup, use a fork to thoroughly mix together the eggs, milk, and salt and pepper to taste. Set aside.

2. Heat a heavy 12-inch nonstick skillet over medium heat, then add the butter and let it melt. Nonstick is the key!

3. Pour in the egg mixture . . .

4. And dot the top with the chopped chiles and pimientos.

5. Here's where things get cool! Lay the slices of bread in the center of the egg mixture . . .

6. Then immediately turn the bread over to the other side. At this point, both sides of the bread are soaked in the egg mixture, and it'll all make sense shortly!

7. Gently shake the pan from side to side to make sure the eggs aren't sticking around the edges, and to keep the bottom of the eggs from burning. Turn down the heat if necessary to keep the eggs from browning too fast.

Inside-out egg sandwich!

8. After the eggs have set for about 2 minutes, use a large spatula to flip the whole round to the other side. (Or if you are feeling adventurous, flip it in the skillet!)

9. So now the eggy bread is cooking on the underside!

10. After 1 minute, lay the pepper Jack slices on the egg directly over where the bread slices are.

11. Using a spatula, fold one side of the cooked egg over the cheese . . .

12. Then do the same with the other side.

13. Slip the spatula squarely under one half . . .

14. And flip it over on top of the other half.

15. Now you just need to think of it as French toast! Let it continue cooking on the first side for a couple of minutes, until golden brown . . .

16. Then flip it over and do the same to the second side. What a sandwich!

17. Remove it to a cutting board and cut it in half with a serrated knife.

18. Serve immediately with ketchup and mustard!

• •

VARIATIONS

» *Leave out the chiles and pimientos for a more traditional bread omelet.*

» *Add a slice of ham over the cheese for more protein.*

Fruity Breakfast Galette

MAKES 6 TO 8 SERVINGS

It's hard to pin down whether this tasty breakfast skillet is actually breakfast (as opposed to dessert) and whether it's actually healthy (I'm gonna go ahead and say yes for my own peace of mind), but it's not really important to pin it down! Just know it's dreamy and easy, too. All you need to do is remember to thaw the pastry in the fridge overnight. From there, everything's gravy.

(To clarify, there is no gravy in this breakfast dish. Figure of speech. Okay, bye.)

1 sheet frozen puff pastry, thawed

1 cup fresh or frozen blueberries, plus more for garnish

1 cup fresh or frozen blackberries, halved, plus more for garnish

1 cup fresh or frozen quartered hulled strawberries, plus more for garnish

¼ cup sugar

2 tablespoons cornstarch

Juice of 1 lemon

3 tablespoons apricot jam

½ cup plain or vanilla Greek yogurt

⅔ cup granola

Maple syrup, for serving

1. Preheat the oven to 425°F.

2. Roll out the puff pastry to thin it out as much as you can . . .

4. In a large bowl, combine the berries, sugar, cornstarch, and lemon juice . . .

6. Spread the apricot jam on the bottom of the crust . . .

3. Then lay it in a 9-inch ovenproof skillet (or you may use a pie plate). Press the pastry lightly into the pan and let the excess hang over a bit (it will shrink during baking).

5. And stir until everything is mixed and the sugar is mostly dissolved.

7. And pour in the berries, scraping the bowl to get everything in.

8. Even out the berries and slide the pan into the oven.

9. Bake the galette until the crust is golden and the berries are bubbling, 30 to 35 minutes. (If the crust starts to get too brown during baking, lightly cover the galette with foil.)

10. Let it cool for about 10 minutes, then top with spoonfuls of yogurt . . .

11. And garnish with fresh berries and granola. Drizzle with maple syrup before serving!

Ranch rainbow!

VARIATIONS

» *Sprinkle with sifted powdered sugar before serving.*

» *Drizzle with honey instead of maple syrup.*

» *Drizzle with (ready?) white chocolate syrup if you just want to totally embrace life.*

Puff pastry and frozen berries make it easy!

Mexican Frittata

MAKES 8 TO 12 SERVINGS

Breakfast doesn't get much easier than a frittata (okay, a doughnut might be a little easier, but . . .). You just pick the fillings, slosh an egg mixture over the top, and cook it! This version really brings the flavors my family loves, and the stovetop-to-broiler method is the fastest way to get your frittata fix!

If you want to be really clever, slice the frittata into strips and fold them inside warm corn tortillas. Mexican frittata breakfast tacos!

2 tablespoons salted butter

8 ounces fresh Mexican chorizo

1 medium red onion, halved and cut into thin wedges

1 red bell pepper, diced

1 orange bell pepper, diced

1 jalapeño, finely diced

2 garlic cloves, minced

2 medium Yukon Gold potatoes, unpeeled, scrubbed, and sliced very thin

1 teaspoon ground cumin

Kosher salt and black pepper

8 large eggs, whisked

¼ cup jarred chunky salsa

½ cup grated Monterey Jack cheese

Fresh cilantro leaves, for serving

1 avocado, diced

1 cup cherry tomatoes, halved

1. Position a rack in the middle of the oven and preheat the broiler.

2. In a large ovenproof skillet, heat the butter over medium-high heat. Add the chorizo and cook, stirring often, until crumbled and completely cooked.

3. Add the onion, both bell peppers, the jalapeño, and garlic . . .

4. And cook, stirring occasionally, until the veggies are starting to soften, about 3 minutes.

5. Add the potatoes, cumin, and salt and black pepper to taste . . .

6. And stir gently until everything is hot, about 2 minutes. Reduce the heat to low.

Finished under the broiler!

7. In a medium bowl, combine the eggs, salsa, Monterey Jack, and salt and black pepper to taste . . .

8. And whisk until well combined.

9. Give the veggies and chorizo one more stir, then pour the egg mixture into the skillet, making sure to get it around the edges.

10. Cook it on the stovetop until the edges are visibly set, 4 to 5 minutes. Place it under the broiler for 5 minutes, watching to make sure it doesn't burn.

11. Cut into wedges, sprinkle with cilantro, and serve with the avocado and tomatoes!

Duke is king of the Drummond dogs.

Leftover Frittata Sandwich

MAKES 8 SERVINGS

I'm obsessed with frittata sandwiches, whether the frittata is left over or made fresh for the occasion. Dijon and arugula give this one a little bit of elegance, and the whole wheat English muffins let you tick off the "healthy" box!

Use any frittata recipe you'd like, but here's a ham and sweet potato version I make time and time again. This frittata uses a more traditional stovetop-oven method, but feel free to use the stovetop-broiler method on the previous page! This is delicious either way.

FRITTATA

12 large eggs

2 tablespoons chopped fresh parsley

2 to 3 dashes hot sauce, plus more for serving

Kosher salt and black pepper

2 tablespoons salted butter

1 cup cubed cooked ham

1 cup frozen sweet potato chunks (or 1 sweet potato, baked until tender, peeled if desired, and cut into ½-inch dice)

FOR SERVING

Whole wheat English muffins

Grainy mustard

Mayonnaise

Small cheddar cheese slices

Hot sauce

Baby arugula

1. Preheat the oven to 375°F.

2. Make the frittata: In a large pitcher or bowl, combine the eggs, parsley, hot sauce, and salt and pepper to taste . . .

3. And whisk until combined. Set aside.

4. In a large ovenproof nonstick skillet, melt the butter over medium-high heat. Add the ham, sweet potato, and salt and pepper to taste . . .

5. And cook, stirring, until everything is hot and the sweet potatoes are starting to turn golden, 3 to 4 minutes. Reduce the heat to low . . .

Not your average Egg McMuffin!

6. And pour in the egg mixture, making sure to get everything around the edges.

9. Cut it into squares/wedges about the size of the English muffins.

12. Serve with fruit salad and dive right on in!

7. Let the frittata cook on the stovetop for 3 minutes, or until the eggs start to set around the edges. Then transfer to the oven to bake until the eggs are just barely set on top, 10 to 12 minutes.

10. To serve: Spread one half of an English muffin with mustard and the other half with mayo. To the bottom half, add a square of cheddar, a piece of frittata, and a dash or two of hot sauce.

8. Let the frittata cool for a few minutes, then slide it out onto a cutting board.

11. Top with baby arugula and the muffin top . . .

FREEZE AND REHEAT

Assemble the sandwiches without the arugula. Let cool, then wrap in aluminum foil and place inside a small freezer bag. Freeze for up to 6 months. To reheat, remove from the freezer bag and foil, then microwave wrapped in a paper towel for 2½ minutes. Add arugula and take on the go!

The English Breakfast Situation

MAKES 4 OR 5 SERVINGS

I fancy myself a proper Englishwoman about 2 percent of the time, solely because of the influence my UK television crew has had on me over the years. I've learned so many things about British culture from my friends: common phrases, the inner workings of Parliament, and (of course) food, and I love every single morsel of info they feed me. I've learned that a true English breakfast spread (known as "The Full English") typically includes bacon, sausage, eggs, mushrooms, tomatoes, baked beans, and toast, and you'll find all of that in this one-and-done skillet. I was sold the first time I tried it! (It's worth mentioning that a curious dish called black pudding is another common component of an English breakfast . . . but my commitment to British culture can only go so far.)

THE SITUATION

3 slices thick-cut bacon, cut into small chunks

5 breakfast sausage links

8 cremini mushrooms, stemmed and quartered

Kosher salt and black pepper

1 cup grape tomatoes

5 large eggs

FOR SERVING

One 28-ounce can baked beans

Fresh parsley leaves, for serving

5 slices bread, toasted and halved

Softened butter

Jam

2. And cook over medium heat, stirring occasionally, until the meat is fully cooked and the mushrooms are deep golden, about 8 minutes. Drain off any excess grease (a little in the pan is okay!).

4. Crack the eggs in any spaces around the pan. (You can move the ingredients aside here and there as you need to.)

1. In a heavy nonstick skillet, combine the bacon, sausage, and mushrooms. Sprinkle with some salt and pepper . . .

3. Add the tomatoes and toss them around to start the cooking process.

5. Sprinkle the eggs with salt and pepper, reduce the heat to medium-low, and shake the pan a bit to keep the eggs from sticking.

English breakfast in a skillet!

6. Meanwhile, in a medium saucepan, heat the baked beans over medium heat so they'll be warm when the skillet is done.

7. Cook the skillet until the whites are set and the yolks are still soft, 5 to 6 minutes. (You can put the lid on the skillet to hasten this along if you wish!) Carefully slide the whole skillet onto a board . . .

8. And sprinkle on parsley leaves.

Serve with the toast, beans, butter, and jam. (And some proper English tea, of course!) Use a spatula to cut individual servings.

No babysitting pancakes at the stove!

Sheet Pan Pancakes

MAKES 12 SERVINGS

This is a lickety-split way to serve a crowd of pancake lovers without having to scoop, flip, and babysit individual pancakes on a griddle. All it takes is a little blender action, then you're just 20 minutes away from fruity (or chocolaty!) pancakes that are golden and glorious!

2½ cups whole milk

2 large eggs

1 tablespoon vanilla extract

2¾ cups all-purpose flour

2 tablespoons baking powder

¼ cup sugar

½ teaspoon kosher salt

8 tablespoons (1 stick) salted butter, melted

1 cup thick-sliced strawberries

1 cup chocolate chips

1 heaping cup blueberries

Butter and warm pancake syrup, for serving

1. Preheat the oven to 425°F.

2. In a blender, combine the milk, eggs, and vanilla . . .

4. Add the flour, baking powder, sugar, and salt . . .

6. Pour in half of the melted butter and pulse a few times to combine.

3. And pulse to mix it well.

5. And blend until smooth, 25 to 30 seconds.

7. Spread 2 tablespoons of the melted butter on a sheet pan, then pour in the pancake batter.

8. Sprinkle the strawberries, chocolate chips, and blueberries over the batter in three sections. Bake until golden on top, about 20 minutes.

9. Brush the remaining 2 tablespoons melted butter over the surface of the pancake. (You won't have this much butter left. Sorry! I like to melt butter in my spare time.)

10. Cut into squares and serve with butter and warm syrup!

· ·

VARIATION

» *Leave the pancake plain, then sprinkle on the toppings after you cut it into squares!*

Kids are fun when they become adults!

Crunchy Breakfast Wraps

MAKES 4 LARGE WRAPS (TO SERVE 4 TO 8)

This is a make-at-home version of Taco Bell's Crunchwrap, the primary benefit being that you can (a) put in it what you wish, and (b) stay at home in your pajamas and not start the car. I love these for hungry teenagers, who can polish off a whole one. I usually opt for a half myself; my teenage days are over!

24 frozen Tater Tot rounds

1 pound bulk breakfast sausage

8 large eggs

¼ cup whole milk

Kosher salt and black pepper

Four 12-inch flour tortillas

1 large avocado, sliced

½ cup halved cherry tomatoes

4 tablespoons jarred pickled jalapeño slices

½ cup grated cheddar cheese

½ cup grated Monterey Jack cheese

4 tablespoons olive oil

Salsa, for serving

Sour cream, for serving

1. Bake the tot rounds according to the package directions. Set them aside. (Don't mind me; I baked extra for "research purposes." Nothing to see here, folks.)

3. Pour the sausage onto a plate lined with paper towels. Return the skillet to the stove and reduce the heat to medium.

5. Pour the mixture into the pan . . .

2. In a large skillet, cook the sausage over medium-high heat until completely crumbled and browned, 7 to 8 minutes.

4. In a small pitcher or bowl, whisk together the eggs, milk, and salt and pepper to taste.

6. And stir until the eggs are cooked to your liking, 3 to 4 minutes. Set the scrambled eggs aside.

Fun for teenagers (and their moms)!

7. Lay down one of the tortillas and arrange one-quarter of the avocado and one-quarter of the tomatoes in the center.

8. Top with 1 tablespoon of the jalapeños and 6 of the tot rounds.

9. Add one-fourth of each of the two cheeses . . .

10. One-fourth of the sausage . . .

11. And one-fourth of the scrambled eggs!

12. Start folding in the sides, overlapping as you go, until the fillings are completely enclosed (it should be a pentagon!). Heat a clean nonstick skillet over low heat and add 1 tablespoon of the olive oil.

13. Place the wrap in the skillet with the edge side down. (This will help it seal!)

14. Cook for 3 to 4 minutes on the first side, making sure it doesn't burn. Flip it over and cook it for another 3 minutes or so on the second side. Repeat to make the other wraps, using 1 tablespoon oil for each.

15. Slice the wraps with a serrated knife . . .

16. And serve them with salsa and sour cream on the side! Wrap them, sliced, in foil for a portable breakfast.

· ·

VARIATION

» *Anything you can put in an omelet or breakfast burrito, you can put in a crunch wrap: bacon, diced ham, green and red bell pepper, diced onion, chopped spinach, mushrooms, different cheeses . . . the works!*

Butter Pecan French Toast

MAKES 6 TO 8 SERVINGS

When I was growing up, French toast meant Wonder Bread dunked in beaten eggs and fried in margarine. And it was absolutely incredible, don't get me wrong. But this is French toast for grown-ups—made with grown-up French bread and a very grown-up caramel sauce spiked with bourbon. Wonder Bread French toast, I love you . . . but I need to run away with this version for a while.

8 tablespoons (1 stick) salted butter, plus more for serving

½ cup whole milk

5 large eggs

1¼ cups packed brown sugar

½ teaspoon ground cinnamon, plus more for serving

1 teaspoon vanilla extract

1 small loaf French bread, cut into 1-inch-thick slices

Pinch of kosher salt

1 cup bourbon (or ½ cup water and ¼ cup milk for a nonalcoholic alternative)

¾ cup chopped pecans

Powdered sugar, for serving

Whipped cream, for serving

1. Heat a large nonstick skillet over medium-low heat and melt 2 tablespoons of the butter.

2. In a large bowl, combine the milk, eggs, ¼ cup of the brown sugar, the cinnamon, and vanilla . . .

3. And whisk until everything's combined and smooth.

4. One by one, dunk the slices of bread into the egg mixture . . .

5. And place them in the buttery skillet.

6. Fit as many slices in the skillet as you can, cooking them until golden on the first side, about 2½ minutes. Flip to cook them on the other side for about 2 minutes.

7. Remove them to a plate. Add 2 tablespoons of the butter to the skillet and repeat with the rest of the bread slices until they're all cooked.

Make the French toast and sauce in the same pan!

8. To the same skillet, add the remaining 4 tablespoons butter, the remaining 1 cup brown sugar, and the salt . . .

9. And stir and cook over medium heat until the butter and sugar are melted and bubbling, 2 to 3 minutes.

10. Turn off the heat completely. Pour in the bourbon and stir, allowing the fumes to dissipate for about 1 minute. Turn the stove on to medium heat . . .

11. And continue to stir and cook for another minute, or until the mixture is starting to thicken.

12. Add the pecans, stir to combine . . .

13. And keep cooking the sauce, stirring constantly, until the mixture is deep golden, 2 to 3 more minutes. Be careful not to cook it too long or it will become chewy! You want a nice caramelly sauce. Turn off the heat.

14. Serve 2 pieces of French toast with a little butter. Sift over some powdered sugar.

15. Spoon on a generous amount of the sauce . . .

16. Then top with whipped cream and a sprinkling of cinnamon.

Breakfast Grilled Cheese

MAKES 1 SANDWICH (WHICH CAN BE SHARED!)

Once upon a time I set out to create a breakfast-friendly grilled cheese. My original idea was to stick a little ham into a normal grilled cheese and call it a day. Next thing I knew, I'd cooked a mile-high sandwich with more cheese and fillings than I knew what to do with.

And it was wonderful!

4 tablespoons (½ stick) butter

6 thin slices deli ham

1 large egg

Kosher salt and black pepper

2 slices swirled pumpernickel rye (or any sliced bread)

1 tablespoon Dijon mustard

1 tablespoon mayonnaise

4 slices Swiss cheese

2 slices tomato

1 thin slice red onion, pulled into rings

1. In a nonstick skillet, melt 1 tablespoon of the butter over medium heat. Bundle up the ham slices and cook them on both sides until browned . . .

3. Add 1 tablespoon of the butter to the skillet and crack in the egg. Sprinkle with salt and pepper and let it cook sunny side up until the white is fully set, about 4 minutes.

5. Lay 2 slices of the Swiss cheese on the mayo slice . . .

2. Then remove them to a plate and set aside.

4. Spread one slice of the bread with the mustard and the other slice with mayonnaise.

6. And top with the browned ham.

7. Lay on the tomato slices and red onion rings.

9. Add the fried egg on top of the onions and bring the sandwich together!

11. Then flip and grill until both sides are golden and the cheese is melted. You might need to reduce the heat to low to ensure the bread doesn't burn!

8. Top the mustard-coated slice of bread with the remaining 2 slices Swiss cheese.

10. In the same skillet, melt the remaining 2 tablespoons butter over medium-low heat. Grill the sandwich on the first side . . .

12. Slice the sandwich in half. Happy breakfast!

This is Duke's ranch. We're all just guests in it.

A definite fork-and-knife situation!

Onion

Ham

Cheese

Tomato

White Chocolate Berry Pancakes

MAKES ABOUT TWELVE 4-INCH PANCAKES

I regret to inform you that these pancakes will ruin you on all other pancakes forever. They are quite literally the most delicious pancakes I have ever made, and I've made a lot of pancakes. For that reason, I would recommend turning the page now and never, ever, *ever* making these.

You have been warned.

1 cup sour cream

2 tablespoons mixed berry jam (any berry jam works!)

2 large eggs

½ teaspoon vanilla extract

2 tablespoons white chocolate syrup, plus more for serving

⅔ cup all-purpose flour

1 heaping teaspoon baking soda

½ teaspoon kosher salt

⅔ cup white chocolate chips, plus more for serving

Butter, for frying and serving

1 cup mixed fresh berries, for serving

Warm maple or pancake syrup, for serving

Canned whipped cream

1. In a large bowl, combine the sour cream, jam, eggs, vanilla, and white chocolate syrup . . .

3. Sift in the flour, baking soda, and salt . . .

5. Add the white chocolate chips . . .

2. And stir until everything just comes together. (Don't overmix!)

4. And gently fold together until almost fully mixed.

6. And fold them in. So, so easy!

Ridiculously delicious!

7. Heat a griddle over medium-low heat and smear it with a little butter. Drop on ¼-cup helpings of batter and cook the pancakes for about 2 minutes on the first side, taking care not to burn them.

8. Flip them over and cook for another 2 minutes. Remove and repeat with the rest of the batter, buttering the griddle before each batch.

10. Sprinkle on the white chocolate chips . . .

B'DAY PANCAKES!

Add 2 tablespoons rainbow sprinkles to the batter and decorate the cooked pancakes with more sprinkles!

9. To serve, arrange the pancakes on a plate and top them with fresh berries, butter, and syrup . . .

11. Then squirt with some whipped cream and add a drizzle of white chocolate syrup. Oh my heavenly pancake goodness!

They're married!

Baked Bagel Egg-in-the-Holes

MAKES 8 SERVINGS

This is a beautiful mess of a breakfast, brunch, lunch, dinner, or midnight feast, and it looks so much more elaborate than it is. It's 100 percent exactly the same well-loved egg-in-the-holes that my husband's grandmother used to make him growing up . . . except these are made on a sheet pan instead of a skillet. And they're baked in the oven instead of fried on the stove. And they're made with bagels instead of bread. And they're served with smoked salmon instead of bacon. And they're topped with hollandaise sauce, red onions, capers, and dill instead of . . . well, nothing. But other than that, they're exactly the same!

The ease of this super-pretty breakfast is that it takes hardly any time to prep for the oven, and you can make the blender hollandaise sauce while they're baking. Feeds a crowd, easy to make, and looks gorgeously inviting? Amen, and *a-men*!

EGG-IN-THE-HOLES

4 everything bagels, sliced

6 tablespoons salted butter, melted

8 medium eggs

HOLLANDAISE

4 medium egg yolks

Juice of 2 lemons, plus more as needed

½ teaspoon cayenne pepper

Pinch of kosher salt, plus more as needed

1 cup (2 sticks) salted butter, melted and very hot

TO SERVE

Kosher salt and black pepper

8 ounces sliced smoked salmon

¼ cup diced red onion

2 tablespoons capers, drained

2 tablespoons chopped fresh chives

1. Preheat the oven to 375°F.

2. Make the egg-in-the-holes: Use a 2-inch round cutter to cut larger holes in the center of each bagel half.

4. Brush the remaining 3 tablespoons butter on the tops of the bagel halves and centers. You want those bagels buttery!

3. Line a sheet pan with parchment paper and brush on 3 tablespoons of the melted butter. Place the bagel halves cut side down, firmly pressing them onto the buttery surface to create a "seal." Lay the centers on the pan, too.

5. Crack an egg into each bagel half. (Don't worry if a small amount of white seeps out from underneath.) Bake for 11 to 12 minutes for a softer yolk or 14 to 15 minutes for a fully cooked yolk. (I wholeheartedly recommend soft!)

So easy and elegant!

6. Meanwhile, make the hollandaise: In a blender, combine the egg yolks, lemon juice, cayenne, and salt . . .

7. And blend for a few seconds to combine.

8. Then, with the blender running, slowly pour in the sizzling hot butter through the lid in a thin, steady stream.

9. Keep pouring until you've added all the butter. You will hear the sauce get thicker and thicker as you pour!

10. Use a spatula to scrape the sides of the blender, then taste and check the consistency. Season with more salt if needed, then add a little more lemon juice if it's too thick. Blend to combine, then put on the lid to keep the sauce warm.

11. Remove the pan from the oven when the eggs reach the desired doneness. (Some of the yolks will be a little cloudy from baking; that's normal!) Sprinkle the eggs with salt and pepper to taste.

12. Carefully transfer the bagels and centers to a large platter (I could only fit six on mine!) and arrange the salmon over the top, tucking it between and under pieces here and there. Sprinkle on the red onion and capers . . .

13. Then pour on some of the hollandaise (save the rest for serving). Or, if you prefer, you can serve all the sauce on the side and let everyone pour to their hearts' content.

14. Sprinkle on the chives and serve while still warm. Beyond beautiful, and so delightful.

VARIATIONS

» *Serve ham, bacon, or sausage instead of salmon, onion, and capers for a more down-home dish.*

» *The bagel egg-in-the-holes are delicious without adornment if you need an easy weekday breakfast!*

Dalgona Coffee

MAKES 2 GENEROUS ICED COFFEE DRINKS
(FOR BREAKFAST OR DESSERT!)

I learned about this whipped coffee beverage the exact same way most of America's population heard about it: on TikTok. It became an overnight sensation during the first few months of 2020, partly because the process of dalgona being made is so satisfying to watch, and partly because there's something about its particular balance of coffee and sugar (and the air bubbles that turn it into the whipped delight) that gives the person drinking it an instant lift in energy, mood, and basic outlook on life.

I will tell you, after making it many times over the past year-plus, that this is another viral recipe that deserves every bit of hype and praise that comes its way.

Note: No need to splurge. Supermarket-quality instant coffee granules will have the best success. Sleeves of fine-ground instant coffee from coffee shops or high-quality instant espresso often don't yield the best results.

1 heaping tablespoon instant coffee granules (see Note)

2 tablespoons sugar

1 tablespoon vanilla extract

1 cup whole milk

1. In a small saucepan or tea kettle, heat some water until very hot. Have it on standby.

2. In a heatproof medium bowl, combine the instant coffee, sugar, and vanilla.

3. Add 2 tablespoons of the hot water and stir to dissolve the ingredients, about 30 seconds.

4. With a hand mixer on medium speed, whip the mixture, moving it around the bowl to introduce as much air as possible.

5. After about a minute, when the dark liquid has begun to turn a deep caramel color, increase the speed to high.

6. Keep whipping for up to 4 minutes or more, until the mixture looks glossy and stiff, like meringue.

7. To make the luscious drink, fill a cup with ice and pour in ½ cup of the milk, leaving about ½ inch of space at the top . . .

Totally worthy of the hype!

8. Then pile on half the whipped coffee! Repeat to make the second drink.

Some folks like to stir it immediately . . . but I love to start sipping immediately and let it mix as I go. So delicious!

And Mauricio makes eight!

Mug Omelets

EACH RECIPE MAKES A SINGLE-SERVING MUG OMELET

As was the case with countless families in the world, the 2020 Covid quarantine meant extra kids and *lots* of extra kitchen mess in my house. After many tears and temper tantrums (mine, not the kids'), I started letting the various members of my household take their daily meal destiny into their own hands. Translation: I told them if they were hungry, they were cordially invited to make themselves something to eat. I couldn't be a line cook in my own house anymore!

Enter: Mug omelets! These saved mornings in our household during those desperate months, but they have absolutely taken hold and become a staple now. They're the fastest way to satisfy your omelet cravings, and the variations are endless. Here are three of my favorites!

Note: Part of the fun of making mug omelets is seeing how much the omelets puff as they cook in the microwave. They immediately start to settle down once you remove them, but trust me—you're in for a laugh. (Not to mention a delightful omelet experience!)

DENVER MUG OMELET

All the classic flavors . . . without the fancy skillet technique!

Butter, for greasing the mug

3 large eggs

2 tablespoons milk

Kosher salt and black pepper

2 tablespoons very finely diced ham

1 tablespoon very finely diced green bell pepper

2 tablespoons grated Monterey Jack cheese

1. Grease the inside of a 12-ounce mug with butter.

3. The milk . . .

5. Use a fork to mix everything until well combined.

2. Add the eggs . . .

4. And a pinch each of salt and black pepper.

6. Add the ham . . .

7. The green bell pepper . . .

9. Mix everything well, wipe the inside upper rim of the mug with a paper towel if it gets too messy, and cook it in the microwave for 90 seconds.

11. Return it to the microwave for another 90 seconds, then carefully remove! Let it sit for 2 minutes before eating.

8. And the Monterey Jack, baby!

10. Carefully remove the mug from the microwave and stir it with the fork to break up any large clumps.

BUILD YOUR OWN!

Other omelet ingredients: pesto, diced tomatoes, crumbled sausage, chopped bacon, caramelized onion, diced avocado, chopped jalapeño!

Denver

Mushroom-Swiss

Southwest

MUSHROOM-SWISS MUG OMELET

My personal fave! The tiny bits of mushrooms are delightful.

Butter, for greasing the mug

3 large eggs

2 tablespoons whole milk

Kosher salt and black pepper

2 cremini mushrooms, very finely chopped

2 tablespoons grated Swiss cheese

4 or 5 baby spinach leaves, very finely chopped

½ teaspoon minced fresh chives

1. Grease the inside of a 12-ounce mug with butter. Add the eggs, milk, and salt and pepper to taste and mix together with a fork.

2. Drop in the mushrooms . . .

3. The Swiss cheese . . .

4. And the spinach and chives.

5. Mix again . . .

6. Clean the upper inside of the mug with a damp paper towel if overly messy, then microwave the omelet for 90 seconds.

7. Carefully remove it from the microwave, then stir with a fork to break up any large clumps.

8. Return it to the microwave for 90 seconds. Wait 2 minutes before eating.

SOUTHWEST MUG OMELET

Zesty, cheesy, and spicy! Serve with blackened tortillas.

Butter, for greasing

3 large eggs

2 tablespoons whole milk

Kosher salt and black pepper

2 tablespoons jarred salsa

2 tablespoons grated Monterey Jack cheese

½ teaspoon thinly sliced green onions

4. Mix, clean the upper inside of the mug with a damp paper towel, then microwave the omelet for 90 seconds.

6. Return it to the microwave for 90 more seconds, and let it rest 2 minutes before eating.

1. Grease the inside of a 12-ounce mug with butter. Add the eggs, milk, and salt and pepper to taste and mix together with a fork. Add the salsa . . .

5. Carefully remove it from the microwave, then stir with a fork to break up any large clumps.

MAKE IT SPICY!

To up the heat factor of the Southwest Mug Omelet, add 1 teaspoon of hot sauce, a pinch of cayenne, and 2 chopped jarred jalapeños to the egg mixture before cooking. Now, *that'll* definitely wake you up!

2. The Monterey Jack . . .

3. And the green onions.

APPS AND SNACKS

If only munchies were a food group! Well, in our house they definitely are, and my snack-loving self wouldn't have it any other way. Whether you're craving a lighter dinner with drinks or building a big ol' table of game food galore, these hearty, tasty nibbles will breathe new life into your appetizer game. Another bonus? Most of these easy dishes can be served with a side salad to make a complete meal! I love food that can adapt to any environment. (I also love wings. And sausage balls. And coconut shrimp. And taquitos. I'll stop spoiling the surprise now—just make sure you keep reading. Yum!)

Irresistibly crispy and crunchy!

Coconut Shrimp

MAKES 6 TO 8 SERVINGS

These are the crispiest, crunchiest, most heavenly fried shrimp you'll ever taste! They're perfect as an appetizer or main course, and even though I'm including a really fast, flavorful dipping sauce, they're so perfectly perfect on their own that I was tempted not to share a sauce at all. (And the truth is, even though I love this sauce, Bryce would dip them in ranch and Todd would dip them in ketchup. To each his own!)

MANGO DIPPING SAUCE

1 cup cubed fresh mango (or jarred mango)

2 tablespoons barbecue sauce

1 tablespoon honey

Juice of 1 lime

½ teaspoon kosher salt

SHRIMP

½ cup all-purpose flour

½ cup cornstarch

2 teaspoons kosher salt

1 teaspoon black pepper

3 large eggs

1 cup sweetened shredded coconut

1 cup panko breadcrumbs

1½ pounds peeled, deveined jumbo shrimp (about 24), butterflied, tails left on

Vegetable oil, for frying

Lime wedges, for serving

Cilantro leaves, for garnish

1. First, make the mango dipping sauce! In a small food processor or blender, combine the mango . . .

3. Lime juice and salt and blend until everything is pulverized.

5. Prepare the shrimp: Create the breading assembly line. Set up three bowls: one with the flour, cornstarch, salt, and pepper mixed together; one with the eggs whisked with ½ cup water; and one with the coconut and panko mixed together.

2. Barbecue sauce, honey . . .

4. Pour the sauce into a dish and set it aside. (You can make this the day before and store it in the fridge!)

6. One by one, bread the shrimp: Dredge the shrimp in the flour-cornstarch mixture and shake off the excess . . .

10. Pour 1 inch of vegetable oil into a skillet and heat over medium heat until it reaches 350°F on a deep-fry thermometer. Add a few of the shrimp and let them cook for 2 minutes on one side . . .

13. And repeat until all the shrimp are fried!

7. Dunk it in the egg mixture . . .

11. Then use metal tongs to turn them over and cook for 2 minutes more, making sure not to burn the coconut.

8. And press it into the coconut breadcrumbs to coat it completely.

12. Remove the shrimp to a plate lined with paper towels . . .

14. Serve the shrimp on a platter with the mango sauce and lime wedges. Sprinkle with cilantro leaves to make it extra fancy!

9. Repeat with the rest of the shrimp!

. . . .

VARIATIONS

» *Use canned peaches instead of fresh mango for a sweet peachy dipping sauce.*

» *Serve the shrimp over rice with the sauce spooned over!*

» *Skip the sauce altogether and serve the shrimp with steak for a surf-and-turf feast.*

Buffalo Chicken Totchos

MAKES 6 TO 8 SERVINGS

In case you haven't heard, totchos are a thing. Basically, you bake frozen tots, then use them to make any variety of "nachos" you happen to have a hankering for. This Buffalo chicken version is spicy, messy, and marvelous!

I recommend having a tall stack of napkins nearby. (And maybe don't eat these on a first date?)

TOTCHOS

1 pound frozen Tater Tots

1½ teaspoons chili powder

½ teaspoon ground cumin

2 tablespoons salted butter

2 boneless, skinless chicken breasts, cut into bite-size pieces

½ teaspoon kosher salt

½ teaspoon black pepper

3 celery stalks, thinly sliced, leaves reserved

2 garlic cloves, minced

2 green onions, thinly sliced

1½ cups cayenne hot sauce (such as Frank's RedHot)

2 cups grated pepper Jack cheese

BLUE CHEESE RANCH

¼ cup blue cheese crumbles

1½ cups Mason Jar Ranch Dressing (page 84) or bottled ranch dressing

Kosher salt and black pepper

1. Preheat the oven to 450°F.

2. Make the totchos: Spread out the frozen tots on a sheet pan, then sprinkle on the chili powder and cumin.

4. While the tots are baking, in a large skillet, melt the butter over medium-high heat. Add the chicken, salt, and pepper . . .

6. Add the celery, garlic, and half the green onions . . .

3. Toss the tots to coat them in the seasoning, then bake them until golden and crisp, 28 to 30 minutes.

5. And stir and cook until the chicken starts to brown, about 3 minutes.

7. And cook, stirring often, until the chicken is cooked through, about 2 minutes.

8. Reduce the heat to low, pour in the hot sauce . . .

9. And stir to coat the chicken. Simmer for another minute, then remove from the heat.

10. Remove the tots from the oven and set the oven to broil. Bunch the tots in a pile in the center of the sheet pan and sprinkle on half the pepper Jack.

11. Pile on the chicken (look how yummy!) . . .

12. Then top with the other half of the cheese. Pop it under the broiler until the cheese is melted, about 3 minutes.

13. Make the blue cheese ranch by stirring together the (wait for it . . .) blue cheese and ranch! (Oh, and salt and pepper, too.)

14. Drizzle some of the blue cheese ranch all over the top, then sprinkle on the celery leaves and the rest of the green onions. Serve with the rest of the blue cheese ranch!

FROZEN TOT IDEAS!

Waffle Tots: Preheat a waffle iron to medium heat and spray with nonstick cooking spray. Fill each well with frozen tots and cook until golden and crisp, about 5 minutes. Serve as hash browns with breakfast or top with bacon, fried eggs, salsa, and avocado.

Tot Hash: Add frozen tots to a nonstick skillet over medium-high heat with diced onion, diced bell pepper, and diced ham. Cook for a few minutes, breaking up the tots into smaller bits as they cook. Continue cooking for 10 more minutes, stirring occasionally, until everything is golden brown. Serve with a sprinkle of parsley.

Chili Cheese Tots: Cook the tots according to the package directions. Top with hot chili, grated sharp cheddar, and diced onion.

VARIATIONS

» *Make traditional totchos by topping the tots with cheddar cheese and cooked taco meat.*

» *Make pizza totchos by topping with marinara, mozzarella, and pepperoni!*

Tots + Nachos =
Totchos!

Taquitos

When I stop at small-town gas stations on road trips with Ladd, I always grab myself a taquito if they have them in their deli case. What could be better than some kind of seasoned meat rolled up in a corn tortilla and fried (that's been sitting under a heat lamp for eighteen hours)?

Nothing. That's what. They're wonderful, and they're great as a snack in front of a football game or served with salad for dinner. Here's my method, which uses leftover chicken tossed in a flavorful sauce. If you have help assembling, they come together pretty quickly!

CHICKEN

2 tablespoons olive oil

1 small onion, sliced

1 tablespoon minced garlic

2 tablespoons ancho chile powder

1 tablespoon ground cumin

1 teaspoon kosher salt

One 8-ounce can tomato sauce

4 cups shredded cooked chicken (see page xxi)

Juice of 1 lime

1½ cups grated Colby Jack cheese

TAQUITOS

Vegetable oil, for frying

18 small corn tortillas

Mason Jar Ranch Dressing (page 84) or bottled ranch dressing, for serving

Salsa, for serving

Shredded lettuce, for serving

Diced tomatoes, for serving

1. First, make the chicken mixture: In a large skillet, heat the olive oil over medium-high heat. Add the onion, garlic, ancho powder, cumin, and salt . . .

2. And stir to start the cooking process and coat the onions in all the spices.

4. Then stir, reduce the heat to medium, and simmer for 5 minutes to slightly reduce the sauce. Turn off the heat.

3. Add the tomato sauce along with ⅔ cup water . . .

5. Add the chicken and stir it to coat . . .

Uses pre-cooked chicken!

6. Then squeeze in the lime juice and set aside to cool. (You can make this mixture up to 2 days in advance and store it in the fridge.)

7. When the chicken is cool, transfer to a bowl and stir in the Colby Jack cheese. This is the filling for the taquitos!

8. Speaking of which, let's make them! Pour 2 to 3 inches oil into a medium Dutch oven and heat it to 375°F on a deep-fry thermometer. Using metal tongs, quickly dunk the tortillas one by one in the oil, letting them fry for 10 to 15 seconds each to make the tortillas easier to work with.

9. Set the tortillas on a paper towel to drain as you go.

10. Using a spoon (or your hands!) spoon about 2 tablespoons of the filling down the middle of a tortilla . . .

11. And roll it up as tight as you can.

12. This is somewhat optional, but I like to secure it closed with a toothpick. Less heartache during frying! Continue assembling the rest of the taquitos.

13. Fry them in batches, 3 or 4 at a time, removing them when the tortilla has turned deep golden, 2 to 3 minutes.

14. Drain them on paper towels as you go and remove the toothpicks after they've drained.

15. Serve them warm on a platter with ranch, salsa, lettuce, and tomatoes.

• •

VARIATION

» *Use leftover pulled pork or shredded brisket in place of the chicken. (Yum!)*

Greek 7-Layer Dip

MAKES 8 TO 12 SERVINGS

My fellow children of the eighties, I know all of you remember seven-layer dip. It was (and still is!) a Mexican-spiced layered dip with refried beans, cheese, guacamole, and all the essentials of life. I will still destroy any seven-layer dip that's placed before me, including this fresh version with all kinds of Mediterranean-inspired goodness. Gimme this and a bottle of wine and I'm putty in your hands!

2 cups hummus

One 16-ounce jar roasted red peppers, drained and roughly chopped

2 cups store-bought tzatziki (cucumber-yogurt dip, sold in the refrigerated dip section)

2 English cucumbers, seeded and cut into medium dice

1½ cups sliced mixed kalamata and Castelvetrano olives

1½ cups crumbled feta cheese

1 pint yellow cherry tomatoes, quartered

Juice of 1 lemon

¼ cup minced fresh parsley

4 soft pita breads, cut into wedges, for serving

Assorted raw vegetables: hollowed and halved mini sweet peppers, sliced radishes, carrot sticks, zucchini sticks, cucumber slices

1. It's all about the layering! In a small baking dish, spread the hummus in an even layer.

3. Spread the tzatziki all over the peppers . . .

5. The olives, which give me a reason to live . . .

2. Sprinkle on the roasted red peppers, spreading them out to completely cover the hummus.

4. Then come the crunchy, beautiful cucumbers . . .

6. The crumbled feta . . .

*Amazing app,
barely any prep!*

7. And the tomatoes!

8. Squeeze the lemon juice all over the top . . .

9. Then add the minced parsley! Yum yum.

10. Serve the dip immediately with pita wedges and/or raw veggies, or cover it with plastic wrap and let it chill for a few hours. It's a great thing to take along to a party!

Be very quiet. We're hunting rabbits.

Made with canned crescent dough! (Don't tell anyone!)

Festive Brie Bites

MAKES 24 BITES

Baked Brie is amazing, but these cute little bite-size versions are even more incredible! I've never found a single one left on the serving plate after a party (and trust me, I've looked), whether I've made a single, double, or triple batch. (And surprise! I use good ol' basic crescent roll dough to make them. Please don't turn me in for this culinary infraction!)

All-purpose flour, for dusting

One 8-ounce can refrigerated crescent dough

Two 5-ounce wheels Brie cheese

3 tablespoons finely chopped dried cranberries

3 tablespoons finely chopped pistachios

1 large egg

1 teaspoon chopped fresh rosemary, plus whole sprigs for garnish

1 teaspoon sea salt

¼ cup pomegranate seeds (optional; great at Christmastime!)

Honey, for drizzling

1. Preheat the oven to 375°F. Line a sheet pan with parchment paper.

2. On a lightly floured surface, unroll the crescent dough and press the seams to seal. Cut the dough into 24 squares and set aside.

4. In a small bowl, combine the dried cranberries and pistachios.

6. And sprinkle the cranberry-pistachio mixture over the cheese.

3. Cut the Brie into 24 pieces, too! (Cut each wheel in 12 pieces, saving the end/rind-heavy pieces for snacking!)

5. Lay a piece of Brie on each square of crescent dough . . .

7. Fold the edges of each square over to connect at the center, pressing them lightly to seal, and lay them seam side down on the parchment.

8. Whisk the egg with 2 tablespoons water and brush the egg wash over each bite.

9. Sprinkle a little rosemary and a little sea salt over each one.

10. Bake until golden, 12 to 14 minutes. Let cool for 2 to 3 minutes.

11. Pile the bites on a plate, garnish with a sprig of rosemary, then, if desired, sprinkle the pomegranate seeds all over the top. Drizzle on honey just before serving.

"Can you give me a ride to the next pasture?"

Baked Brie with Mushrooms

MAKES 8 SERVINGS

Whether made in small bites or *en croûte*, as in this recipe, baked Brie is a true wonder, and even though it's often only seen at holiday celebrations, it really is a year-round decadence. The secret is how easy it is to make; it's a no-brainer! I like to add red wine to mine, because (a) I love red wine and (b) I love red wine.

(Wait . . . did I say that twice?)

1 tablespoon olive oil

1 tablespoon salted butter

½ medium onion, cut into medium dice

2 garlic cloves, minced

½ pound cremini mushrooms, sliced

1 tablespoon minced fresh rosemary

2 teaspoons minced fresh thyme

Kosher salt and black pepper

½ cup red wine (such as Cabernet)

All-purpose flour, for dusting

1 sheet frozen puff pastry, thawed

One 8-ounce wheel Brie cheese

1 large egg

Mini sweet peppers, halved and seeded, for serving

Crackers, for serving

Edible flowers, for garnish (optional)

1. Preheat the oven to 375°F. Line a sheet pan with parchment paper.

2. In a large skillet, heat the oil and butter over medium-high heat. Add the onion, garlic, mushrooms, rosemary, thyme, and a pinch each of salt and pepper.

3. Cook the mushrooms, stirring often, until they start to turn golden, 5 to 6 minutes.

4. Pour in the wine, stirring constantly . . .

5. And cook until the wine is mostly absorbed and evaporated.

6. Pour the mushrooms onto a plate and set them aside to cool.

7. Lightly flour a work surface and lay out the puff pastry. Stretch it just a bit to flatten, then spoon the mushrooms in the center.

8. Lay the Brie wheel on top of the mushrooms . . .

9. Then fold up the corners and edges of the pastry and seal them . . .

10. Into a neat little package!

11. Flip the package over onto the parchment so that the seam side is down. Whisk the egg with 2 tablespoons water and brush the egg wash all over the pastry . . .

12. And sprinkle with a little salt.

13. Bake until deep golden, 30 to 32 minutes. Serve with peppers and crackers, cutting into the pastry right after serving. (Decorate with edible flowers and/or herbs if you wish!)

Super elegant, super simple!

Baked Wings with Habanero Honey

MAKES 4 TO 6 SERVINGS

These wings are not messin' around in the spice department, just to let you know. Habaneros will light your soul on fire if you're not careful! However, if you can handle the heat, these sweet-and-sticky (and spicy!) wings will rock your world. The heat does subside just a tad as the sauce cooks, but you are cordially invited to use sliced jalapeños (or jarred, if you like) instead of habaneros.

I guess I like to walk on the wild side sometimes. It's a good thing I always have milk in the fridge!

WINGS

2½ pounds chicken wing sections

2 teaspoons kosher salt

1 teaspoon black pepper

1 teaspoon smoked paprika

HABANERO-HONEY SAUCE

1 cup honey

1 tablespoon barbecue sauce

1 tablespoon Louisiana hot sauce

3 tablespoons apple cider vinegar

2 or 3 habanero peppers, thinly sliced and seeds removed (can use jalapeños for less heat!)

FOR SERVING

¼ cup chopped fresh cilantro

Mason Jar Ranch Dressing (page 84) or bottled ranch dressing

1. Preheat the oven to 400°F. Line a sheet pan with foil, then place a wire rack on the pan.

2. Prepare the wings: Lay the wing pieces on the rack and sprinkle both sides with the salt, pepper, and smoked paprika. Bake for 25 minutes.

4. Add the sliced habaneros. Then go wash your hands!

3. Meanwhile, make the habanero-honey sauce: In a small saucepan, combine the honey, barbecue sauce, hot sauce, and vinegar.

5. Stir to combine and bring to a gentle boil over medium heat. Reduce the heat to low and simmer, stirring occasionally.

"Fried" in the oven!

6. Remove the chicken from the oven and turn over the wings using tongs. Return the pan to the oven for another 20 minutes.

8. Remove the chicken from the oven and turn on the oven broiler. Dunk the wings one by one in the sauce, completely coating them, returning them to the wire rack as you go.

7. By this time, the sauce will be luscious! Remove it from the heat.

9. Place the wings under the broiler until the coating is a bit caramelized, about 3 minutes. (Watch to ensure the wings don't burn!)

10. Serve warm with a sprinkle of cilantro and ranch dressing on the side.

Nothing like an Oklahoma sunrise!

Fried Pasta Chips

MAKES 4 SERVINGS

Instead of writing some kind of witty paragraph to introduce this recipe, I really need only say what the recipe is. It's a simple two-word phrase that rolls off the tongue with poetic grace, and it will change your snack life for the better. Are you ready? Here goes . . .

Fried pasta.

And the people said "Amen!"

Vegetable oil, for frying

8 ounces bow-tie pasta

Kosher salt

1 teaspoon dried basil

1 teaspoon dried thyme

1 teaspoon dried rosemary

1 teaspoon dried oregano

1 teaspoon garlic powder

½ teaspoon red pepper flakes

½ teaspoon black pepper

Warm marinara sauce, for serving

2 tablespoons grated Parmesan cheese

Chopped fresh parsley, for garnish

1. Pour about 2 inches of oil into a large Dutch oven and heat over medium heat to 375°F on a deep-fry thermometer.

3. Use paper towels to blot as much moisture off the pasta as you can, then let it sit for 5 minutes or so to finish drying.

5. And process to a really fine powder, about 1 minute.

2. Cook the pasta in lightly salted water according to the package directions until very tender, not too al dente. Drain well and spread out on a parchment-lined sheet pan.

4. Make the amazing spice mix. In a small food processor (or a regular blender!), combine the basil, thyme, rosemary, oregano, garlic powder, pepper flakes, black pepper, and 1 teaspoon salt . . .

6. Transfer the powder to a small bowl.

7. When the pasta is totally dry and the oil is to temperature, use a spider or slotted spoon to transfer batches of it to the oil.

9. Remove the pasta when it's golden and crisp . . .

11. While the batch of pasta is still warm, sprinkle with the seasoning mix and toss to coat. Repeat until all of the pasta has been fried and spiced.

8. Immediately move the pasta around as it fries, breaking it up as you can. (It will stick together in clumps, which is normal!)

10. And drain it on paper towels. You can use the tool to break up any clumps that have formed!

12. Serve the fried pasta with the marinara and sprinkle the Parmesan and parsley on top!

They're letting Alex catch dinner tonight!

Fried bow ties!
My favorite!

Stepped-Up Sausage Balls

MAKES ABOUT FORTY-EIGHT 1-INCH SAUSAGE BALLS

I have a great love for appetizers I remember from the 1970s, and sausage balls take up a whole lot of that space in my brain. This is very close to the original version (which uses baking mix as a binder, natch!), but since I can't leave well enough alone, I spiked these with some chiles and other kinds of fun.

My original recipe for these called for twice the ingredients (and therefore twice the yield), so I halved it to save myself from myself. I think I'm going to have to halve it again, because the sausage balls really are that hard to resist!

1 pound spicy breakfast sausage (such as Jimmy Dean or J.C. Potter)

2 cups grated Monterey Jack cheese

One 4.5-ounce can chopped green chiles

One 4-ounce jar diced pimientos, drained

¼ medium onion, finely grated

Pinch of kosher salt

½ teaspoon black pepper

¼ teaspoon chili powder

2 tablespoons minced fresh parsley, plus more for serving

¾ cup baking mix (such as Bisquick)

Mason Jar Ranch Dressing (page 84) or bottled ranch dressing, for serving (optional)

Barbecue sauce, for serving (optional)

1. Preheat the oven to 400°F. Line a sheet pan with foil.

2. In a large bowl, combine the sausage, Monterey Jack, green chiles, pimientos, onion, salt, pepper, chili powder, and parsley.

3. Add the baking mix . . .

4. And stir until everything is well combined.

5. Scoop into tablespoon-size portions . . .

6. And roll them neatly between your hands.

1979 called—they want
their sausage balls back!

7. Place them on the prepared sheet pan . . .

8. And bake until golden brown, 20 to 22 minutes. You should see a little bit of crust on the tops!

9. Sprinkle them with more parsley and serve with ranch or barbecue sauce.

Pa-Pa sighting! (He's doing great these days.)

The Fiery Goat

When I first made this super-easy appetizer, I thought I'd try a bite or two before going about my day. I was wrong. Before I knew it, I had stood at my kitchen counter and "taste-tested" a good one-quarter of the pan, accompanied by a bottle of white wine (some of which had gone into this dish's sauce, yum yum). And okay, it was about half the pan. But it wasn't my fault! Turns out, soft, melty goat cheese with a golden broiled crust atop spicy tomato and red pepper sauce is one of my weaknesses. Who knew?!

1 tablespoon olive oil

1 medium onion, diced

2 garlic cloves, grated

1 teaspoon smoked paprika

1 teaspoon Italian seasoning

½ teaspoon red pepper flakes

1 cup dry white wine (or chicken or vegetable broth)

One 10-ounce jar roasted red peppers, drained and finely chopped

One 14.5-ounce can diced tomatoes with basil, garlic, and oregano

Kosher salt and black pepper

One 8-ounce log fresh goat cheese, cut into eight 1-inch discs

1 tablespoon minced fresh parsley

1 tablespoon grated lemon zest

Crostini, for serving

1. In a 10-inch ovenproof skillet, combine the olive oil, onion, and garlic. Stir over high heat for 1 minute.

3. And stir and cook until the onion starts to soften, another 3 minutes.

5. Add the roasted peppers and tomatoes, along with a dash each of salt and black pepper . . .

2. Add the smoked paprika, Italian seasoning, and pepper flakes . . .

4. Pour in the wine and let it reduce for 1 minute, stirring often.

6. And stir and cook until most of the liquid has cooked off, about 10 minutes. Remove the pan from the heat and preheat the oven broiler.

7. Add the slices of goat cheese, lightly pressing them into the sauce.

8. Broil until the cheese is deep golden brown, 2 to 4 minutes, watching to make sure the cheese and sauce don't burn.

9. Sprinkle on the parsley and grate some lemon zest on top. Serve with crostini, and prepare to be amazed!

The Fiery Hill!

Warning: The Fiery Goat is impossible to resist!

SALADS

Over the past year, I came to the stark realization that I have spent the greater part of my adult life in a salad rut. Oh, I'd occasionally whip up some kind of special-occasion salad here and there if the mood would strike, but it would take a scientific calculator to tally up the number of iceberg-and-ranch situations I've gotten myself into over the past decade or so. It's okay—it happens! But fortunately, something recently clicked and I've been working hard to re-ignite my salad life with a vengeance. Okay, that sounded a little harsh. What I mean is, the list of salads you're about to behold will make you fall in love with salads all over again, starting with my go-to handful of mason jar dressings to big, beautiful salads that are so good it's hard not to eat the whole darn bowl. Salad ruts, begone!

Tahini

Ranch

Greek

Raspberry

Italian

My five faves!

Mason Jar Dressings

EACH DRESSING MAKES 2 TO 2½ CUPS

I've used mason jars to make salad dressing far more times than I've used them for canning. If I had to actually whisk or stir salad dressing ingredients together, I swear I'd get cranky! These five incredible (and versatile!) dressings are all shaken, not stirred, and you can use them for all your salad, dipping, and marinade needs. I couldn't possibly pick my favorite of the five, and that's why I'm sharing them all with you.

(These are all made in a 1-quart mason jar; the wide-mouth jars make it easier.)

MASON JAR ITALIAN DRESSING

Classic and tangy, with garlic, seasonings, and Parmesan texture. This is a good basic vinaigrette for any salad, or a light marinade for chicken!

Try me in Big Festive Salad (page 96) and Italian Chopped Salad (page 101).

1¼ cups olive oil

¼ cup white wine vinegar

2 tablespoons balsamic glaze (or balsamic vinegar if you prefer)

1 tablespoon sugar

Pinch of kosher salt

Pinch of black pepper

1 tablespoon Italian seasoning

3 tablespoons grated Parmesan cheese

1. In a 1-quart mason jar, combine the oil, vinegar, balsamic glaze, sugar. salt, pepper, and Italian seasoning.

2. Sprinkle in the Parmesan.

3. Screw on the lid and shake vigorously for 30 seconds, or until well combined! Taste and adjust the seasonings. Store in the fridge for up to 2 weeks.

MASON JAR RANCH DRESSING

My classic herby ranch, which is suitable for everything from iceberg salads to Buffalo wings! We go through this stuff by the gallon, and we aren't sorry!

Try me in Baked Wings with Habanero Honey (page 68), Buffalo Chicken Totchos (page 53), Classic Stromboli (page 147), Salad Bar Salad (page 88), Stepped-Up Sausage Balls (page 74), and Taquitos (page 56).

¼ cup buttermilk

¼ cup whole milk, plus more for thinning

½ cup mayonnaise

¼ cup sour cream

3 dashes hot sauce

2 teaspoons distilled white vinegar

¼ teaspoon paprika

1 garlic clove, minced

2 tablespoons minced fresh parsley

2 teaspoons chopped fresh dill

1 teaspoon chopped fresh oregano

Pinch of kosher salt

Pinch of black pepper

1. In a 1-quart mason jar, combine the buttermilk, whole milk, mayonnaise, and sour cream.

2. Add the hot sauce, vinegar, paprika . . .

3. The garlic, parsley, dill, oregano, salt, and pepper.

4. Screw on the lid and shake vigorously for 30 seconds, thinning with milk if needed to get it to really mix. Taste and adjust the seasonings. Store it in the fridge for up to 2 weeks.

MASON JAR TAHINI DRESSING

Tahini is a smooth sesame paste sold in jars, and it's one of the main ingredients in hummus. The first time I tried a salad dressing made with tahini, I was a little miffed I'd been missing out on it all these years. This dressing is creamy and a little different, and it's perfect on pretty much any salad you have in front of you!

Try me in Sheet Pan Salad (page 94).

1 cup tahini

¼ cup olive oil

2 tablespoons honey

Juice of 1 lemon

1 garlic clove, pressed through a press

1 teaspoon Dijon mustard

½ teaspoon kosher salt, plus more to taste

Pinch of black pepper

1. Scrape the tahini into a 1-quart mason jar.

4. Screw on the lid and shake the jar vigorously for 1 minute . . .

5. Or until very creamy and smooth. Taste and adjust the seasonings. Store in the fridge for up to 2 weeks.

2. Add the olive oil, honey, lemon juice . . .

3. And ⅓ cup water and the garlic, mustard, salt, and pepper.

MASON JAR GREEK DRESSING

A light vinaigrette with Greek seasonings and the double tang of lemon juice and red wine vinegar. The perfect dressing for Greek salad (naturally) or as a marinade for grilled vegetables.

Try me in Roasted Greek Salad (page 91).

1½ cups olive oil

4 garlic cloves, grated

Juice of 2 lemons

3 tablespoons red wine vinegar

2 tablespoons fresh oregano

1 tablespoon za'atar seasoning (or any Mediterranean seasoning)

Kosher salt and black pepper

1. In a 1-quart mason jar, combine the olive oil and garlic.

2. Squeeze in the lemon juice . . .

3. And add the vinegar.

4. Sprinkle in the oregano, za'atar seasoning, and salt and pepper to taste.

5. Screw on the lid and shake for 30 seconds, or until everything is well mixed. Store in the fridge for up to 2 weeks.

MASON JAR RASPBERRY DRESSING

Pretty and pink, this vinaigrette has juicy bits of raspberries and a little Dijon. It's my new favorite salad dressing, and I predict you'll fall in love!

Try me in Market Basket Salad (page 104) and So-Good-for-You Salad (page 107).

½ cup fresh raspberries, smashed

1 tablespoon honey

1 cup olive oil

½ cup raspberry vinegar or red wine vinegar

1 teaspoon Dijon mustard

Kosher salt and black pepper

1. In a 1-quart mason jar, combine the raspberries and honey . . .

4. Then add ¼ cup water and salt and pepper to taste.

5. Screw on the lid and shake vigorously for 30 seconds, or until the dressing is well mixed. Store in the fridge for up to 2 weeks.

2. And use the handle of a wooden spoon to smash the raspberries until they're mostly broken up.

3. Add the vinegar and the mustard.

Salad Bar Salad

MAKES 6 TO 8 SERVINGS

Salad bars crack me up, because they really aren't about the salad at all—but about what tonnage of non-salad ingredients you can put on a few obligatory bites of lettuce. This main-dish salad celebrates all that is wonderful (and nondietetic) about American salad bars in a fun and beautiful way!

1 large head romaine lettuce, sliced into 1-inch pieces

½ English cucumber, halved lengthwise and thinly sliced

1 small red onion, thinly sliced

1 cup grated cheddar cheese

4 hard-boiled eggs, cut into chunks

Kosher salt and black pepper

½ cup grated or julienned carrot

1 cup frozen peas, thawed

8 slices bacon, cooked to crisp and roughly chopped

1 cup halved grape tomatoes

Mason Jar Ranch Dressing (page 84) or your favorite bottled ranch

1. Place the lettuce in a wide, shallow bowl and add the toppings in piles! The cucumber . . .

3. The grated cheddar . . .

5. Then come the carrots . . .

2. The red onion . . .

4. And the hard-boiled eggs. Sprinkle them with salt and pepper.

6. The peas (please!) . . .

There's lettuce under there! Promise! ☺

7. And the bacon and tomatoes!

8. Serve with ranch dressing on the side . . .

9. Or drizzle some dressing all over the top.

· ·

VARIATION

» *Try topping with avocado, small broccoli florets, potato salad (yes!), sesame seeds, diced bell pepper, diced ham, shaved turkey, feta cheese, black olives . . . I could go on and on!*

SHOP THE SALAD BAR!

Supermarket salad bars have always been a clever way to buy small amounts of various veggies, meats, and jarred condiments for those times you don't want to buy a whole bushel or container—and for those times you need to grab ingredients for a super-fast last-minute meal! Here are three great ways to shop the salad bar:

Stir-Fry Veggies: Select sliced onions and bell peppers, baby corn, and mushrooms. Just cook the protein you want and throw in the already prepped veggies!

Cole Slaw: Grab two colors of shredded lettuce, shredded carrots, and onions! Top with a mild dressing such as oil and vinegar or even an herby ranch. Toss when you get home!

Egg Salad: Combine diced hard-boiled eggs, bacon, green onions, and other add-ins. Add a creamy dressing and toss when you get home!

Roasted Greek Salad

MAKES 6 TO 8 SERVINGS

I am 100 percent on board with this new genre of sheet pan salads. They're incredibly delicious and go something like this: Roast some of the ingredients (usually vegetables and protein) until browned and flavorful. Let everything cool for a bit, then dump on a bunch of cold, fresh ingredients and toss with dressing. It's a best-of-both-worlds salad scenario, and sometimes in the dead of winter, when the world is a sea of brown and there's nothing growing in my garden but desolation, I try to see how many different varieties of sheet pan salads I can come up with.

Here's one of my favorites. I enjoy it as a main dish, but it's a great side with grilled beef, chicken, or fish!

2 cups red and yellow cherry tomatoes

2 red bell peppers, cut into large chunks

Two 7-ounce blocks feta cheese, cut into large cubes

1 cup Mason Jar Greek Dressing (page 86)

3 lemons, halved lengthwise

2 English cucumbers, seeded and thickly sliced on the diagonal

1 cup pitted kalamata olives

1 small red onion, thinly sliced

¼ cup fresh dill fronds

1. Preheat the oven to 475°F.

2. Place the tomatoes, bell peppers, and feta on a sheet pan. Drizzle with ¼ cup of the dressing . . .

3. And toss to coat the veggies and feta.

4. Lay the lemon halves cut side up all over the pan.

5. Roast until the veggies and feta start to brown, 17 to 19 minutes. Feel free to stick them under the broiler for 2 minutes to get more color.

6. Let everything cool for 15 minutes, then squeeze one of the roasted lemon halves into the remaining dressing.

7. Shake the dressing to emulsify it and pour half of it over the veggies and feta.

8. Add the cucumbers . . .

9. The red onion and olives . . .

10. And toss everything to mix the ingredients and coat them in dressing. (You can toss in the roasted lemons or use them for garnish.)

11. Arrange everything on a large platter and top with the fresh dill. Serve the rest of the dressing on the side!

VARIATIONS

» *Use Halloumi cheese in place of the feta.*

» *Top the finished salad with shaved Parmesan.*

» *Omit the red bell peppers and add a jar of drained sliced roasted red peppers after roasting.*

» *Toss with cooked and cooled farfalle pasta for a big pasta salad!*

Paige and Walter: forever friends!

Amazing flavor— and so easy!

Sheet Pan Salad

MAKES 8 SERVINGS

This sheet pan salad is hard to put into words, but I'll try: I roast squash and cauliflower (which is a favorite veggie combo of mine) with shallots and chickpeas, then use the roasted veggies as a base to build a serious looker of a salad. It's a showstopper, actually. Creamy tahini dressing really makes it unique, but this salad is so pretty and delicious, you could top it with ranch and it'd still be a star!

1 small Delicata squash, halved lengthwise, seeded, and sliced crosswise into ¼-inch-thick half circles (or acorn squash)

2 cups cauliflower florets

½ butternut squash, cut into ½-inch cubes (about 2 cups)

3 small shallots, thinly sliced (or 1 small red onion)

One 15.5-ounce can chickpeas, drained and rinsed

¼ cup olive oil

2 teaspoons Italian seasoning

Kosher salt and black pepper

4 cups baby arugula

2 ounces crumbled goat cheese

¼ cup pomegranate seeds (or dried cranberries or cherries)

¼ cup pistachios (pecans or walnuts would be great, too!)

¾ cup Mason Jar Tahini Dressing (page 85) or your favorite bottled dressing

1. Preheat the oven to 450°F.

2. Lay the Delicata squash, cauliflower, butternut squash, shallots, and chickpeas on a sheet pan. Drizzle on the olive oil. Sprinkle with the Italian seasoning and salt and pepper to taste . . .

3. And toss the veggies until everything is coated in the oil and seasonings.

4. Roast the veggies until the edges are starting to brown, about 25 minutes.

5. Let the veggies sit for 10 minutes to cool slightly (or you can let them cool to room temperature if you prefer!), then pile on the arugula.

6. Sprinkle on the goat cheese, pomegranate seeds, and pistachios!

7. Drizzle on the tahini dressing. Serve it right on the sheet pan!

Build the salad on top of roasted veggies!

Big Festive Salad

MAKES 8 TO 10 SERVINGS

I first made this showstopper of a salad around Christmastime one year, and it's perfect for the holidays, with the candied nuts and the jewel tones of radicchio and pomegranate seeds. But dang it if this isn't a perfect salad at any time of year, so don't let it languish in the "Holiday Recipes" tab of your recipe box.

Does anyone even have recipe boxes anymore? Boy oh boy, I certainly hope so.

Great for holidays or year-round!

CANDIED NUTS

¼ cup raw pistachios

¼ cup chopped raw hazelnuts (or cashews or almonds!)

2 tablespoons packed brown sugar

1 teaspoon kosher salt

½ teaspoon vanilla extract

SALAD

5 cups salad greens of your choice (arugula, spinach, whatever you prefer)

2 cups quartered and sliced radicchio or red cabbage

½ cup dried cranberries

½ cup fresh blueberries

3 mandarin oranges, peeled and segmented

½ cup pomegranate seeds (I buy them as seeds—much easier!)

¼ cup freshly grated Parmesan cheese

1 cup Mason Jar Italian Dressing (page 83) or bottled Italian dressing

1. Make the candied nuts: In a nonstick skillet, toast the pistachios and hazelnuts over medium-high heat to a nice medium brown, 4 to 5 minutes, occasionally shaking them in the pan.

2. Reduce the heat to low, add the brown sugar, salt, vanilla, and 1 tablespoon water . . .

3. And cook for about 1 minute, stirring constantly, until the sugar has dissolved and the nuts are coated.

4. Pour them onto a parchment-lined sheet pan and let them cool for at least 10 minutes.

5. Build the salad: Place a small dish in the center of a round board or platter. Arrange the greens and radicchio around the dish, then sprinkle on the dried cranberries and blueberries.

6. Arrange the mandarin slices all over the top.

7. Sprinkle on the pomegranate seeds.

8. Lightly sprinkle the Parmesan over everything (around Christmastime this looks like snow!).

9. Sprinkle on the candied nuts and pour the dressing into the dish. Gorgeous!

Arty Bread

MAKES 6 TO 8 SERVINGS

Bread counts as salad in my world!

There's a trend in food these days that involves pressing edible items—usually a mix of vegetable pieces, herbs, and olives—onto bread dough to form recognizable scenes. The bread bakes and looks like a piece of art every time. I've seen flower gardens, rainbows, wheelbarrows—heck, my Food Network friend Molly Yeh even made bread art depicting her young daughter, Bernie! I find it all beautiful (and very delicious), but the version I make is a little more dumbed-down, which . . . well, makes sense. Frozen bread dough makes this a really easy thing to try again and again.

1 pound frozen white bread dough, thawed according to the package directions

1 cup halved red and yellow cherry tomatoes

½ cup pitted olives

2 tablespoons fresh sage leaves

6 to 8 small rosemary sprigs

½ small red onion, thinly sliced

3 tablespoons olive oil

½ teaspoon flaky sea salt

2 tablespoons finely grated Parmesan cheese

1. Preheat the oven to 450°F.

2. Lay the bread dough in an ungreased 9 x 13-inch pan. (I used a quarter sheet pan.) Use your hands to stretch and press it into the corners.

4. Arrange the tomatoes and olives evenly on the dough, pressing lightly to anchor them. Upside down, right side up—there's no right or wrong method!

6. Add red onion slices in the gaps.

3. Dimple the surface using your fingers. It's focaccia-esque fun!

5. Press the sage and rosemary in between the tomatoes and olives.

7. Lightly press all the ingredients into the dough again . . .

Made with frozen bread dough!

8. Then generously brush the surface with the olive oil . . .

9. And sprinkle with the sea salt and Parmesan.

(Psst. I tried a flower garden. Couldn't help myself.)

10. Bake the bread until golden brown, 22 to 25 minutes. Slice it into squares and savor every bite! (Abstract art has always been my preference!)

- -

VARIATION

» *Top with your favorite combination of pepper rings, sliced black olives, fresh dill sprigs, flat-leaf parsley leaves, asparagus tips, jarred jalapeño slices, Broccolini florets, chives.*

FROZEN BREAD DOUGH FOR THE WIN!

Frozen bread dough is a staple I can't imagine being without. It's sold in two forms: standard loaves and individual dinner rolls. It usually requires a good 3 to 4 hours for it to thaw and rise, but I just move the dough from the freezer to the fridge at night. By dinnertime the next day, it's thawed and ready to make your favorite carby recipes:

Pizza: Roll out into a large oval and place on an ungreased sheet pan. Top with anything you like, then bake at 425°F for 15 to 18 minutes, until golden and bubbly!

Calzone: Roll out into smaller circles, fill with cheese and other pizza toppings, then fold over and seal. Brush with an egg wa   nd bake at 400°F for 23 to 25 minutes, until golden and bubbly!

Breadsticks: Roll out nd b   generously with butter. Sprinkle on garlic salt and grated Parmesan, then press them   ly into the dough. Slice into sticks, separate them on a sheet pan, and bake at 425°F for 15) 18 minutes.

Italian Chopped Salad

MAKES 4 TO 6 SERVINGS

We serve this salad at my restaurant P-Town Pizza, and it's my favorite salad in the world. Mounds of chopped jarred staples, fridge proteins, and fresh produce make this salad an absolute feast for the senses, and it never gets old for me! Prep everything in advance so when it comes time to assemble the salad, it moves lightning fast.

3 cups chopped romaine

1 cup multicolored cherry tomatoes, halved

1 small English cucumber, seeded and diced

1 small red onion, diced

One 15.5-ounce can chickpeas, drained and rinsed

1 cup jarred sliced pepperoncini, drained

½ cup diced jarred roasted red peppers

1 cup cubed mozzarella cheese

½ cup jarred (or canned) artichoke hearts, quartered

1 cup sliced green olives

1 cup chopped salami

1 cup chopped pepperoni

½ cup fresh basil leaves, some reserved for garnish

1 cup Mason Jar Italian Dressing (page 83), plus more to taste

1 cup freshly grated Pecorino Romano cheese, plus more for serving

1. In an oversize bowl, combine the romaine, tomatoes, cucumber, onion, chickpeas, pepperoncini, and roasted red peppers.

2. Add the mozzarella . . .

3. The artichoke hearts . . .

4. The olives . . .

5. And the salami and pepperoni.

6. Drop in most of the basil leaves.

7. Pour in ½ cup of the dressing . . .

9. Sprinkle in ¾ cup of the Romano . . .

11. Mound individual servings on plates, sprinkle on more cheese . . .

8. And stir/toss until it's all coated.

10. Then toss and give it a taste. Add a little more dressing as desired!

12. And garnish with the reserved basil leaves!

Me and Alex,
Alex and me.

Just prep, dump, dress, and toss!

Market Basket Salad

MAKES 1 GENEROUS SALAD

Whether you serve it in a nifty wood box or on a simple dinner plate, this salad is a work of art—not to mention an easy, healthy treat to make for yourself or for friends! It isn't fancy at all in the ingredients or the prep—it just looks that way.

Looks can be deliciously deceptive.

3 large green leaf lettuce leaves

¼ cup frisée or other light, tender greens

½ small cucumber, halved and thinly sliced

3 sweet baby peppers, halved and seeded, stems left on

1 watermelon radish (or 3 regular radishes), thinly sliced

4 ounces fresh mozzarella cheese, sliced

4 ounces prosciutto, thinly sliced

4 or 5 grape tomatoes, halved

Kosher salt and black pepper

¼ cup Mason Jar Raspberry Dressing (page 87) or your favorite bottled vinaigrette

Good-quality store-bought breadsticks, for serving

1. In a food-safe box or on a plate or platter, lay down one or two of the lettuce leaves as a foundation.

3. Add the mozzarella slices . . .

5. Add the tomatoes in whatever gap you can find.

2. Prop up the third lettuce leaf, then add the frisée, cucumber, baby peppers, and radish slices. (Have fun with your own arrangement!)

4. And the prosciutto slices, bundling them up as you add them so they look ruffly.

6. Sprinkle the mozzarella with salt and pepper . . .

A special (but simple) salad!

7. And spoon a little of the vinaigrette over the mozzarella.

8. Serve with breadsticks and more vinaigrette. Make it a finger food salad for yourself or share it with a friend on two plates. You deserve it!

TODD AND ALEX

Alex was seven when Todd was born, and while all the Drummond sibs have their areas of common ground, these two have a special bond that warms their ol' mom's heart. With that many years of age difference, there's no competing for position or fighting like close siblings tend to do. There's just the tenderness Alex feels for her brother, whom she remembers as a newborn, and the regard Todd has for his sister, who went to college (and grew up) when he was just eleven. Based on their sweet relationship alone, I would recommend that all mothers put seven years between all their children. However, in my case that would have meant having babies over about thirty years . . . so *never mind*!!

So-Good-for-You Salad

MAKES 8 TO 10 SERVINGS

When I first made this salad, I had challenged myself to create a truly healthy salad that my mom, a retired oncology social worker, would put her stamp of approval on. Well, lo and behold—I did it! My mom loved this salad, full of all the healthy greens, nuts, and proteins our bodies long for. And besides all the "it's healthy" stuff . . . the combination of ingredients really is so delicious and satisfying.

In the interest of full disclosure, I would like to share that I do sometimes fantasize about putting this salad inside a flour tortilla and making it a wrap. With a few slices of Swiss cheese. And honey mustard to dip it in. And a side of fries . . .

⅓ cup walnut halves

⅓ cup slivered almonds

⅓ cup pistachios

Pinch of kosher salt

3 large collard green leaves, stems and midribs removed

1 bunch Tuscan (lacinato kale), stems and midribs removed

1 bunch Swiss chard, stems and midribs removed

2 cups baby spinach

¾ cup Mason Jar Raspberry Dressing (page 87) or your favorite salad dressing, or more to taste

⅓ cup canned kidney beans, rinsed

⅓ cup canned chickpeas, rinsed

6 ounces crumbled feta cheese

⅓ cup sunflower seeds

1. In a dry skillet, toast the walnuts, almonds, and pistachios over medium heat until medium brown, 2 to 3 minutes, shaking the pan occasionally. Remove the pan from the heat and sprinkle the nuts with the salt. Let cool for 10 minutes.

2. Roll up the collard green leaves and slice them into ribbons.

4. Pour in the dressing . . .

3. Do the same with the kale and Swiss chard. Place all the greens, including the spinach, in a large bowl.

5. And toss to completely coat the greens.

Ree's mom approves!

5. Sprinkle on the toasted nuts . . .

8. The feta cheese . . .

7. The kidney beans and chickpeas . . .

9. And the sunflower seeds! Serve with extra dressing on the side.

GOOD INGREDIENTS

These salad add-ins have the most bang for your buck, nutrition-wise! Experiment in a big bowl to find your favorite variety:

Kale, spinach, asparagus, sunflower seeds, pumpkin seeds, walnuts, broccoli, cauliflower, carrots, cooked quinoa, pistachios, kidney beans, garbanzo beans, black beans, crumbled feta, grated hard cheddar, hard-boiled eggs, avocado, cooked flaked salmon.

Best mom ever!

SOUPS AND STEWS

❦

Louis P. De Gouy said that soup is "cuisine's kindest course." Mr. De Gouy was correct. No one feels worse after eating a bowl of soup; I have seen this human truth play out time and time and time again at the table in my kitchen. Even if your day is crumbling all around your ankles, all the chaos and strife is suspended, if not eliminated, after a little soup-eating session. I have found that there's a common misconception about soup out there: That in order to make good soup, you have to devote many hours to perfecting the flavors and letting it simmer. I haven't found that to be the case at all, thank goodness, and this list of soups (with an easy cheese toast thrown in for good measure) can go from pot to bowl in far less than an hour, and some even faster than that. Now that's souper news!

There are
11 cans in there!

11-Can Soup

MAKES 8 SERVINGS

This soup shouldn't be as delicious as it is. It's a dump-and-stir sensation of a soup that's only as complicated as using your can opener. (You don't even have to drain anything!) This particular combination of ingredients somehow just works; it's total witchery if you ask me! And you can simmer it for a minimum of 30 minutes if you need to get it on the table fast . . . but the longer you can let it go, the richer the flavor. I love to "pair" (this makes things sound more sophisticated; thank you for not laughing) the soup with cheesy toast.

Now go forth and open cans!

One 16-ounce jar sliced roasted red peppers

One 14.5-ounce can diced tomatoes with garlic and basil

One 15-ounce can tomato sauce

One 15-ounce can cannellini beans, undrained

One 15-ounce can Great Northern beans, undrained

One 15-ounce can chickpeas, undrained

One 15-ounce can minestrone soup

One 14.25-ounce can cut Italian green beans

One 14-ounce can quartered artichoke hearts

One 8-ounce can sliced mushrooms, pieces and stems

One 6-ounce jar prepared pesto

1 tablespoon dried parsley flakes

¼ teaspoon Italian seasoning

Salt (optional)

Grated Parmesan cheese, for serving

Easy Cheesy Toast (page 114), for serving

1. Make the soup: Open all the cans and jars first so you're ready to roll. And here's something cool: no draining! That's part of the awesomeness.

2. Dump the roasted peppers, diced tomatoes, tomato sauce, cannellini beans, Great Northern beans, chickpeas, minestrone, green beans, artichoke hearts, and mushrooms into a large soup pot or Dutch oven.

3. Add the pesto. You won't regret it.

4. Sprinkle in the dried parsley and Italian seasoning . . .

5. And stir everything together. Bring to a boil over medium-high heat, then reduce the heat to low and simmer for at least 30 minutes . . . 1 hour if you have the time! (And yes . . . I should have used a larger pot. I love an adventure, I guess.)

6. Taste the soup for seasoning, adding a little salt if needed. Look how delicious!

7. Ladle it up and serve with grated Parmesan and Easy Cheesy Toast! (I had to help myself to 2 pieces . . . actually, I couldn't help myself. Ha ha.)

EASY CHEESY TOAST

MAKES 8 TOASTS

This effortless cheese toast can be made with any combination of bread and cheese you have in your life (or your pantry/fridge).

8 slices ciabatta bread

1½ cups grated mozzarella cheese

8 teaspoons grated Parmesan cheese

1 teaspoon Italian seasoning

16 slices provolone cheese

1. Preheat the oven broiler. Meanwhile, lay the ciabatta slices on a sheet pan (Note: I used two separate pans for the cheese toast!) and sprinkle the mozzarella evenly over each slice. Sprinkle on the Parmesan and Italian seasoning . . .

2. Then fold the slices of provolone and lay 2 slices on each slice of bread. (I told you this toast was cheesy!)

3. Broil until the cheese is bubbling and starting to get brown around the edges, 3 to 4 minutes. Watch carefully so the toasts don't burn!

Speedy Dumpling Soup

MAKES 6 SERVINGS

This delightful soup is almost too good to be believed, both because of how easy it is and because of its sheer tastiness. I've made it several times and have always enthusiastically devoured it, but on the day I cooked the batch of soup you see in these photos, as I sat down on what happened to be a very cold day to enjoy the fruits of my labor, I thought to myself that it had to be in the top ten most delicious soups I've ever tasted. It really is that good!

Once you read the ingredients and steps below, you will probably have your doubts . . . so all I can do is paraphrase Nike in order to convince you: *Just try it.*

6 cups low-sodium chicken or veggie broth

2 garlic cloves, minced

1 tablespoon grated fresh ginger

¼ cup reduced-sodium soy sauce

2 cups broccoli slaw (about half a 12-ounce bag)

1 red bell pepper, thinly sliced

2 green onions, thinly sliced, dark greens and light greens separated

One 16-ounce bag frozen pork or veggie dumplings or pot stickers

Sriracha

1. Pour the broth into a large soup pot or Dutch oven over medium-high heat. Glug glug glug!

2. As it begins to heat up, add the garlic and ginger . . .

3. And the soy sauce. Stir and bring everything to a gentle boil.

4. When the broth starts bubbling away, add the slaw . . .

5. The strips of bell pepper . . .

6. And the light parts of the green onions. Give everything a stir . . .

7. Then add the dumplings straight outta the freezer!

8. Reduce the heat to low and simmer until the veggies and dumplings are tender, 8 to 10 minutes. Squeeze in sriracha to taste! (I add about 3 tablespoons, because I love excitement.)

9. Serve with the darker parts of the green onions sprinkled on top!

He cleans up nice!

Uses frozen dumplings and broccoli slaw!

Cheesy Tomato Soup

MAKES 6 SERVINGS

Close your eyes and imagine French onion soup, with all its indulgent melted-under-the-broiler cheesiness. Now imagine a tomato-cheddar version. Too heavenly to even think about, isn't it?

Well, open your eyes! It's reality! And it's about to rock your world.

1 thin baguette, sliced into 12 rounds

¼ cup olive oil

2 tablespoons salted butter

1 yellow onion, diced

4 garlic cloves, minced

1 tablespoon minced fresh thyme leaves

1 tablespoon minced fresh oregano leaves

Kosher salt and black pepper

2 tablespoons tomato paste

¾ cup white wine (or chicken or vegetable broth)

One 32-ounce bottle tomato juice

Two 14.5-ounce cans stewed tomatoes

3 tablespoons sugar

1 cup heavy cream

½ cup freshly grated Parmesan cheese

½ cup freshly grated Pecorino Romano cheese

⅓ cup chopped fresh basil, plus more for serving

12 small slices cheddar cheese

1. Preheat the oven to 375°F.

2. Lay the baguette slices on a sheet pan and generously drizzle them with the olive oil. Bake until slightly toasted and crisp, about 8 minutes. Set aside.

3. In a heavy pot, melt the butter over medium-high heat. Add the onion, garlic, thyme, oregano, and a sprinkling of salt and pepper.

4. Stir and cook until the onion starts to turn translucent, about 5 minutes.

5. Add the tomato paste and stir to coat the onions. Let it start to cook, about 1 minute.

6. Pour in the wine! My favorite part.

French onion soup . . .
tomato–cheddar style!

7. Next come the tomato juice and the stewed tomatoes . . .

10. Then add the Parmesan, Romano (feel free to just use more Parmesan to keep it simple!), and basil.

13. Place a bowl on a sheet pan. Lay 2 of the baguette crisps on top of the soup and add a slice of cheddar to each slice.

8. Then the sugar (to counteract the acid in all the tomato products!) . . .

11. Stir and bring the soup to a boil, then reduce the heat to low and simmer for 10 minutes. Taste and adjust the salt and pepper as needed.

14. Transfer the pan to the broiler and broil until the cheese melts, 1½ to 2 minutes. Watch carefully!

9. And finally the cream. Stir to combine . . .

12. Preheat the oven broiler, then ladle the soup into broilerproof bowls.

15. Garnish the soup with the basil. (Use caution when serving, as the bowl will be hot!)

White Chicken Chili

When I used to imagine white chicken chili, I would picture a dish that had to cook and simmer for well over an hour to get the flavors to develop. But then I discovered the truth: White chicken chili is actually a really quick, incredibly easy dinner—particularly when you use rotisserie chicken to speed things along! The flavor of this one-pot dish is big and bold, and it'll take approximately one bite for it to become a family favorite.

3 tablespoons olive oil

1 medium onion, diced

4 garlic cloves, minced

1 generous tablespoon Tex-Mex or taco seasoning

3 cups shredded cooked chicken (see page xxi)

Two 4-ounce cans chopped green chiles, undrained

Two 15-ounce cans cannellini beans, drained

4 cups (1 quart) low-sodium chicken broth

Hot sauce (such as Cholula or Tabasco)

2 tablespoons masa harina (corn flour, sold in the Hispanic foods aisle)

½ cup heavy cream

One 10-ounce bag frozen fire-roasted corn (no need to thaw)

Kosher salt

Sour cream, for serving

1 avocado, sliced

2 cups grated Monterey Jack cheese

2 limes, cut into wedges

1. In a soup pot or Dutch oven, heat the olive oil over medium-high heat. Stir in the onion and garlic, sprinkle in the Tex-Mex seasoning . . .

2. And cook, stirring often, until the onion starts to soften, about 3 minutes.

3. Add the chicken, stir to combine . . .

4. And add the green chiles . . .

5. The beans . . .

6. And the chicken broth.

Another rotisserie chicken winner!

7. Add a few (or several!) dashes of hot sauce . . .

11. Pour the masa mixture into the soup . . .

15. Serve topped with sour cream, avocado, hot sauce, and Monterey Jack. Have lime wedges for squeezing. Yum yum!

8. And stir. Bring the mixture to a gentle boil.

12. Then stir and let the chili cook and thicken for about 10 minutes.

9. In a measuring cup, combine the masa and heavy cream . . .

13. When the chili is thick and bubbling, add the corn . . .

10. And stir with a fork into a thick paste.

14. And stir it until the corn is hot, about 2 minutes. Taste and add salt and more seasonings if needed!

MAKE IT IN THE SLOW COOKER!

This white chicken chili can be made in the slow cooker, and it's ridiculously easy! Simply combine the onion, garlic, seasoning, chicken, green chiles, beans, broth, hot sauce, masa paste, corn, and salt in a slow cooker. Cover and cook for 4 hours on high, 8 hours on low. Stir and adjust the seasonings, then serve as above, with sour cream, avocado, cheese, lime wedges, and extra hot sauce. So incredibly easy—it's my favorite kind of slow cooker recipe! (If I have to pre-brown the chicken or cook anything before adding it to the slow cooker, it makes me cranky.)

Brocco-flower Soup

MAKES 8 TO 10 SERVINGS

I love a good broccoli-cheese soup, but this one brings in a bit of cauliflower to make things interesting! This is an absolutely luscious veggie soup, and it uses two forms of broccoli: fresh florets and frozen broccoli pieces. The florets give the soup a fresh broccoli flavor, but the bag of frozen pieces is a super-cheap, easy way to bulk up the soup. (No need to use all fresh when you're going to puree it anyway!)

Feel free to use all fresh broccoli or all frozen, however—the soup is great any way you slice it. (I mean ladle it!) It's nice to have options in the kitchen.

6 tablespoons salted butter

1 large head broccoli, cut into very small florets

1 large head cauliflower, cut into very small florets

1 medium onion, diced

2 garlic cloves, minced

3 tablespoons all-purpose flour

3 cups vegetable broth, plus more as needed for thinning

2 cups whole milk

½ cup half-and-half

One 12-ounce bag frozen broccoli cuts

½ teaspoon smoked paprika

¼ teaspoon cayenne pepper

Kosher salt and black pepper

3 cups grated cheddar cheese

One 4-ounce jar pimientos

½ cup jarred sliced hot cherry peppers

2 tablespoons minced fresh parsley, plus parsley leaves for garnish

1. In a large soup pot, melt 3 tablespoons of the butter over medium-high heat. Add the fresh broccoli and cauliflower. Stir and cook until the veggies start to get tender, 3 to 4 minutes.

3. Add the remaining 3 tablespoons butter to the pot along with the onion and garlic. Cook, stirring, until the onions start to turn translucent, about 3 minutes.

2. Remove half of them to a bowl and set aside.

4. Sprinkle in the flour . . .

Uses fresh and frozen broccoli!

5. And stir for another minute, so that the flour coats the veggies and starts to cook.

6. Mix in the broth . . .

7. Then the milk and half-and-half! Mmmm.

8. Dump in the frozen broccoli pieces . . .

9. Then add the smoked paprika, cayenne, and salt and black pepper to taste. Stir to combine!

10. Cover the pot, reduce the heat to medium-low, and cook, stirring occasionally, for 18 to 20 minutes, until the broccoli is soft.

11. Remove the lid and reduce the heat to low. Use an immersion blender to completely puree the soup. You can also let it cool and puree it in batches in the blender if you have the time.

12. Add the reserved broccoli and cauliflower (you can save back a few pieces for garnish!), the cheddar, pimientos, and sliced cherry peppers.

13. Stir and cook until the cheese is melted and the soup is hot. If you'd like it thinner, you can splash in more broth to your liking.

14. Stir in the parsley. Serve hot, garnished with a few whole parsley leaves.

· ·

VARIATIONS

» *Stir in 3 chopped Roma tomatoes at the very end, with the parsley.*

» *Serve in a bread bowl!*

Tuscan Chicken Soup

MAKES 8 SERVINGS

This soup has hearty chunks of chicken and tomatoes, but if I'm being honest, the bread is what's so delicious about it. I mean . . . *yum*! But the other stuff is important, too—and in fact, the whole darn experience of this soup is just marvelous and memorable. It's rustic and really quick to make, but it still feels special!

(Oh, and there's bread in it. Did I happen to mention that?)

8 thick slices sourdough bread

2 tablespoons olive oil, plus more for toasting the bread and serving

2 tablespoons salted butter

3 boneless, skinless chicken thighs, diced

1 small yellow onion, finely diced

2 garlic cloves, minced

2 tablespoons tomato paste

One 28-ounce can tomato puree

One 14.5-ounce can diced tomatoes

One 15-ounce can cannellini beans, drained

4 cups (1 quart) low-sodium chicken broth

2 teaspoons chopped fresh oregano leaves, plus more for garnish

2 tablespoons honey

One 6.5-ounce jar marinated artichoke hearts, drained

Kosher salt and black pepper

½ cup shaved Parmesan cheese, for serving

1. Preheat the oven to 425°F.

2. Lay the bread slices on a sheet pan and drizzle them generously with some olive oil.

4. In a soup pot or Dutch oven, heat the olive oil and butter over medium-high heat. Add the chicken . . .

6. And cook, stirring occasionally, until the chicken is fully cooked, about 5 minutes.

3. Bake until golden and crisp, about 10 minutes. Set aside.

5. Then add the onion and garlic . . .

7. Add the tomato paste and stir it in . . .

8. Then add the tomato puree, diced tomatoes, cannellini beans . . .

9. The broth . . .

10. The oregano and honey . . .

11. And stir. Reduce the heat to medium-low, bring to a simmer, and cook for 10 minutes to combine the flavors.

12. Add the artichoke hearts . . .

13. And season with salt and pepper to taste! Stir and heat, then taste to make sure the seasonings are just right.

14. To serve, tear the bread into large chunks and place in the bottom of soup bowls.

15. Ladle the soup over the bread, letting the chunks stick up on the surface.

16. Top with Parmesan shavings and garnish with fresh oregano. Drizzle with olive oil.

Sprinkle with a little more pepper and enjoy every slurp!

STEP IT UP!

Turn this soup into a French onion situation: Preheat the oven broiler. Ladle the soup over the bread in an ovenproof bowl, then lay two slices of mozzarella on top. Broil until golden and bubbly.

VARIATIONS

» *Leave out the chicken and use veggie broth for a vegetarian soup.*

» *Add ½ teaspoon red pepper flakes for a spicier soup. Yum!*

» *Use herb garlic bread to add a little more flavor to the mix.*

Creamy Mushroom Soup

MAKES 8 SERVINGS

If you don't like mushrooms, you need to flee the scene immediately. There are mushrooms before, during, after, under, over, and in this soup. I should have called it Mushroom Preposition Soup!

And actually, don't leave just yet. Because this is one mushroom recipe that will win you over from the dark side. Creamy, dreamy, and easy! (Oh . . . and shroomy.)

4 tablespoons (½ stick) salted butter

1½ pounds white button mushrooms, sliced

Kosher salt and black pepper

1 medium onion, diced

4 garlic cloves, minced

2 celery stalks, thinly sliced

Leaves from 2 thyme sprigs

2 tablespoons all-purpose flour

¾ cup sherry

5 cups vegetable broth

½ cup heavy cream

2 teaspoons balsamic vinegar

Balsamic glaze, for serving

Minced fresh parsley, for serving

1. In a large pot, melt 2 tablespoons of the butter over medium-high heat. Add one-third of the mushrooms . . .

3. Then remove the mushrooms from the pot and set them aside for serving.

5. Reduce the heat to medium and add the rest of the mushrooms, the thyme, and salt and pepper to taste.

2. And cook, stirring occasionally, until dark golden brown, about 5 minutes. Season with salt and pepper to taste . . .

4. Add the remaining 2 tablespoons butter to the pot, along with the onion, garlic, and celery. Cook, stirring often, until the onion starts to soften, about 2 minutes.

6. Cook, stirring frequently, until the vegetables are soft, 5 to 6 minutes.

Mushrooms everywhere you turn!

7. Sprinkle the flour over the vegetables . . .

8. And stir constantly for about 3 minutes, to cook the flour.

9. Pour in the sherry and stir . . .

10. Then add the broth.

11. Let the soup cook until the mushrooms are tender and the flavors have developed, about 20 minutes.

12. Use an immersion blender to puree the mixture to the consistency you'd like.

From high school QB . . .

13. I like to go all the way, but you can stop when there are still large chunks of mushrooms if you prefer!

15. And the balsamic vinegar. Stir and taste the soup, adjusting the salt and pepper as needed.

14. Pour in the cream . . .

16. Ladle up the soup . . .

17. Then pile the browned mushrooms in the center. Drizzle with balsamic glaze and sprinkle parsley on top.

To college QB!

Ramen Soup with Saucy Shrimp

MAKES 6 TO 8 SERVINGS

This is one of my favorite recipes in this cookbook, or any cookbook! The flavors are all there, from the ginger to the tiny shrimp coated in chili sauce. But the ease with which this luscious noodle dish comes together is delicious in itself, and it's one of those dishes you'll find yourself making again and again, just because you can! (And just because it's one of the best things you've ever tasted in your life . . . no exaggeration.)

SAUCY SHRIMP

1 pound frozen cooked salad shrimp, thawed

¼ cup Thai sweet chili sauce

2 tablespoons minced fresh cilantro

SOUP

2 tablespoons salted butter

1 red bell pepper, sliced

1 jalapeño, finely diced

1 small onion, thinly sliced

3 garlic cloves, grated

2 tablespoons grated fresh ginger

One 13-ounce can full-fat coconut milk

5 cups vegetable broth, plus more as needed

1½ teaspoons ground turmeric

1 cup frozen cut green beans

Two 3-ounce packages ramen noodles (any flavor), seasoning packs discarded

Juice of 1 lime, or more to taste

2 tablespoons soy sauce

1 tablespoon sriracha, or more to taste

¼ cup each fresh cilantro and basil leaves, plus more for garnish

1. Make the saucy shrimp: In a small bowl, combine the shrimp and sweet chili sauce.

2. Toss to combine, making sure all the shrimp are coated . . .

3. Then sprinkle on the minced cilantro.

4. Make the soup: In a large deep skillet or pot, melt the butter over medium-high heat. Add the bell pepper, jalapeño, and onion . . .

5. And cook, stirring constantly, until the vegetables start to brown, 2 to 3 minutes. Add the garlic and ginger . . .

6. The coconut milk . . .

Packaged ramen is the secret.

7. The vegetable broth . . .

8. And the turmeric and stir to combine.

9. Cook until everything is hot and close to boiling, about 5 minutes.

10. Add the green beans . . .

11. And the ramen noodles . . .

12. And stir until the noodles are submerged. Reduce the heat to medium-low and let the soup simmer until the noodles are just starting to get tender, 5 to 7 minutes.

13. Turn off the heat and add the lime juice . . .

14. The soy sauce and sriracha . . .

15. And the cilantro and basil.

16. Stir and taste, adding more sriracha if you'd like more spice! Splash in more broth if you'd like the soup to be a little thinner (it naturally thickens as it cooks).

17. Serve generous portions, then spoon the saucy shrimp over the top.

18. Garnish with more cilantro and basil leaves!

White Lasagna Soup

MAKES 6 TO 8 SERVINGS

The most complicated part of making this creamy, dreamy veggie soup is slicing a pound of mushrooms. If you've got that under control (which you do), you can have this incredibly tasty soup on the table within 30 dang minutes. No-cook lasagna noodles and luscious ready-to-go adornments make it not only lightning fast but deliciously elegant!

I wish I had a bowl of this in front of me right now. I would totally go be alone with it.

¼ cup olive oil

1 pound white button mushrooms, sliced

1 tablespoon fresh thyme leaves

1 teaspoon kosher salt

2 teaspoons Italian seasoning

3 garlic cloves, minced

3 tablespoons all-purpose flour

6 cups (1½ quarts) low-sodium vegetable broth

1 cup heavy cream

8 ounces no-boil lasagna noodles

4 cups (one 5-ounce package) baby spinach

Ricotta cheese, for serving

Prepared basil pesto, for serving

1. In a Dutch oven or other soup pot, heat the olive oil over medium-high heat. Add the mushrooms, thyme, and salt . . .

3. Until the mushrooms have released their liquid and turned nice and brown.

5. Reduce the heat to medium and sprinkle in the flour . . .

2. Then stir and cook for 6 to 8 minutes . . .

4. Add the Italian seasoning and garlic and cook, stirring, for another minute to release the flavors.

6. Then stir for another minute to cook the flour a bit.

7. Pour in the broth, then stir, bring to a simmer, and cook until the mixture thickens, 10 minutes or so.

10. When it's hot and bubbling, break up the lasagna noodles and add them in pieces . . .

13. And stir until the spinach is wilted.

8. Pour in the cream. (My favorite part!)

11. And stir and cook the noodles until they're al dente. It'll just take about 3 minutes!

14. Ladle the soup into bowls, add dollops of ricotta and drizzles of pesto, and serve!

9. Stir and return the soup to a simmer.

12. Finally, add the spinach . . .

VARIATIONS

» *Pour in ⅓ cup white wine or sherry before you add the broth.*

» *Add shredded cooked chicken with the noodles for some extra protein!*

» *Add diced bell pepper with the mushrooms.*

MASH UP YER SOUP!

Lasagna plus soup is just my kind of mathematical mash-up! So what other well-known recipes out there can be made into a soup? Well . . . I lie awake at night obsessing over that very thing.

Tacos: Make taco soup! Ground beef, taco seasoning, tomatoes, broth, and all the good stuff. Top with corn chips, cheese, sour cream, and hot sauce . . . just like you would tacos!

Cheeseburgers: Make cheeseburger soup! Ground beef, onions, tomatoes, broth, simmer, then stir in a little processed cheese with lots of cheddar. Serve and top with diced tomatoes and cubes of sesame seed buns.

Jalapeño Poppers: Make jalapeño popper soup! Take the easy road and simmer a mix of broth, cream of chicken soup, cream cheese, chopped bacon, and jarred jalapeños. Top with cheddar. Delicious!

Made in 30 minutes!

PIZZA AND SANDWICHES

I love carbs. Specifically, bread. More specifically, bread involving lots of melted cheese. Enter this carbalicious collection of pizzas, flatbreads, sandwiches, and stromboli that will open your eyes and your heart to some pretty awesome possibilities. Think of these recipes as blueprints, and just use the various methods to sub in your own ingredients and express your creativity! A range of different breads is used in order to demonstrate the lengths I will go to in order to find all the different carb-packed vessels available to mankind. My teenage boys and their football friends like to tell one another to "get that bread," which roughly means "go out and win." I prefer to think it refers to pizza and sandwiches. I'm a cool mom that way.

A broccoli-cheese celebration!

Broccoli-Cheese Stromboli

MAKES 6 TO 8 SERVINGS

I love researching the origin of popular dishes. Before I dove into the history of stromboli—which is basically pizza wrapped up in a roll, then sliced—I had a gut feeling I'd discover that it didn't actually hail from Italy, as is the case with several Italianish Americanish recipes. And it turns out that stromboli was actually invented in Philadelphia, by an Italian American named Nazzareno Romano. But I also learned that Mr. Romano may have gotten the name for the dish from an Ingrid Bergman/Roberto Rossellini film called (get this) *Stromboli*!

The search for fun facts such as this is exactly the reason that I can't remember to make an appointment for Todd to get his driver's license.

Anyway, this is a broccoli-cheese version of what is usually a meaty masterpiece (see Classic Stromboli, page 147), and I think it's one of the best kid-friendly things ever.

3 tablespoons olive oil

1 tablespoon salted butter

1 medium yellow onion, thinly sliced

2 garlic cloves, minced

1 head broccoli, cut into small florets

Kosher salt and black pepper

All-purpose flour, for rolling out the dough

One 1-pound loaf frozen bread dough, thawed

¼ cup sun-dried tomato pesto

1 cup grated cheddar cheese

8 slices mozzarella cheese

8 fresh basil leaves

¼ cup grated Parmesan cheese

Jarred marinara sauce, warmed

1. Preheat the oven to 400°F. Oil a sheet pan with 1 tablespoon of the olive oil and set aside.

2. In a large skillet, heat the butter and 1 tablespoon of the olive oil over medium heat. Add the onion and garlic and cook, stirring often, until the onion starts to soften, about 3 minutes.

3. Add the broccoli, season with salt and pepper . . .

4. And cook, stirring often, until the broccoli has softened and started to turn bright green, another 2 minutes. Remove from the heat and set aside.

5. Lightly flour a work surface and roll the bread dough into a large rectangle about 11 x 13 inches.

9. Shingle the mozzarella slices over the cheddar . . .

13. Fold over the final side . . .

6. Spread the pesto all over the dough, leaving about a 1-inch border all around.

10. And lay the basil leaves all over the mozzarella.

14. And turn the roll over so that the seam side is down, taking care not to tear or stretch the dough.

7. Top the pesto with the broccoli mixture . . .

11. Fold in the short sides . . .

15. Use a sharp knife to slice 5 vents across the top.

8. Sprinkle on the cheddar . . .

12. Then bring one long side toward you . . .

16. Brush the surface with the remaining 1 tablespoon olive oil . . .

17. And sprinkle with the Parmesan. This bakes into a delicious crust!

18. Carefully transfer the stromboli to the baking sheet . . .

19. And bake until the crust is deep golden brown, 23 to 25 minutes.

• •

VARIATIONS

» *Add finely diced seasoned grilled chicken to the onion and broccoli mixture.*

» *Add a layer of whole roasted red peppers over the broccoli mixture.*

» *Serve with ranch instead of marinara!*

20. Let the stromboli sit for about 5 minutes, then slice it and serve it with warm marinara sauce.

Happy birthday, Fred and Rusty!

Classic Stromboli

MAKES 6 TO 8 SERVINGS

This is a more classic, meat-a-licious version of stromboli that's stuffed with deli cuts and provolone. It's a must-make for any football-related watch party, especially one that teenagers will be attending. (Don't leave out the pepperoncini—they make the stromboli sing!)

2 tablespoons olive oil

One 1-pound loaf frozen bread dough, thawed

⅓ cup prepared pesto

6 ounces thinly sliced salami

6 ounces thinly sliced capicola or prosciutto

6 ounces large pepperoni slices

8 slices provolone cheese

8 fresh basil leaves

½ cup drained pepperoncini, chopped

⅓ cup grated Parmesan cheese

Mason Jar Ranch Dressing (page 84) or bottled ranch dressing or warmed marinara, for serving

1. Preheat the oven to 400°F. Oil a sheet pan with 1 tablespoon of the olive oil and set aside.

2. Lightly flour a work surface and roll the bread dough into a large rectangle about 11 x 13 inches.

4. Lay the salami in a line down the center, overlapping the slices.

6. The pepperoni . . .

3. Spread the pesto all over the surface, leaving a 1-inch border all around.

5. Do the same with the capicola . . .

7. And the provolone!

8. Lay the basil leaves on top of the cheese . . .

9. And sprinkle the pepperoncini over the basil.

10. Fold in the short sides . . .

11. Then fold up one of the long sides . . .

12. And roll it up to enclose all the ingredients. Turn it seam side down.

13. Use a sharp knife to slice 5 vents across the top.

14. Brush the surface with the remaining olive oil . . .

15. And sprinkle on the Parmesan.

16. Bake until deep golden, 23 to 25 minutes.

17. Let the stromboli sit for about 5 minutes, then slice and serve with ranch dressing. (Look at that cheese!)

GET CREATIVE!

Other calzone fillings: sautéed mushrooms, chopped black olives, Canadian bacon or ham, roasted red peppers, sliced red onions!

Steak Sandwich (or Salad!) Board

MAKES 4 TO 6 SERVINGS

I love multipurpose kitchen tools, and I really love multipurpose recipes! This is a brilliant way to put your guests' dining destinies into their own hands, and every time I make this I feel a teeny bit clever. Sliced steak is served on a board with grilled onions, dressing, bread, and fixins. Everyone can decide whether they want to build a sandwich or just a big, beautiful salad!

"Both" is also a suitable option.

Two 1-pound rib-eye steaks (¾ inch thick)

Kosher salt

2 tablespoons lemon-pepper seasoning

¼ cup olive oil

2 large onions, sliced into ½-inch-thick rounds

½ cup sour cream

½ cup mayonnaise

3 tablespoons prepared horseradish

1 teaspoon Worcestershire sauce

½ teaspoon black pepper

1 head green or red leaf lettuce, leaves separated

2 tomatoes, sliced

6 ounces white cheddar cheese, sliced

1 loaf crusty bread, sliced

2 green onions, dark-green tops only, sliced

Chips, for serving (optional)

1. Preheat a grill pan over medium-high heat. (Or light the outdoor grill!)

2. Season both sides of the steaks with salt and the lemon-pepper seasoning.

3. Oil the grill pan with the olive oil, then lay the steaks and onions on the pan.

4. Grill the onions until they're tender but not falling apart, about 5 minutes per side. Grill the steaks for about 4 minutes per side for medium-rare, 3 minutes per side for rare. Remove them and let them rest under foil.

5. In a medium bowl, whisk the sour cream, mayonnaise, horseradish, Worcestershire, and black pepper until smooth. Set aside.

Build a sandwich or a salad!

6. Slice the steak (mine's on the rare side!) into strips. Cut away the larger pieces of fat if you prefer.

7. Arrange the steak and onions on a pretty board with the lettuce, tomatoes, cheddar, bread, and dressing. Sprinkle the steak and dressing with green onions before serving.

Have guests build their own sandwich (look at the glory!) or, if they prefer, a salad.

Me, enjoying not cooking. Ha!

Pantry Pizza Pronto

MAKES TWO 8-INCH PIZZAS

This is a brilliantly tasty pizza that can be made almost entirely from pantry staples. The only exception is the cheese, but I always have that in abundance in my fridge . . . so the makings of this beautiful pizza are almost always at my fingertips!

One 8-inch store-bought focaccia round

½ cup jarred marinara sauce

2 cups grated provolone (or mozzarella) cheese

3 ounces dry-cured sausage (such as saucisson sec), thinly sliced (about 16 slices; you can even use summer sausage from that Christmas gift box from last year!)

½ cup quartered artichoke hearts

2 tablespoons sliced kalamata olives

½ cup drained deli-sliced hot cherry peppers

2 tablespoons drained sliced Manzanilla olives with pimientos

¼ cup grated Parmesan cheese

¼ cup prepared pesto

Small fresh basil leaves

1. Preheat the oven to 425°F.

3. Lay the two halves cut side up on a sheet pan and spread the marinara sauce on both pieces.

6. Arrange the cherry peppers and green olives in between the artichoke hearts. Transfer to the oven . . .

4. Top the pizzas with the grated provolone, then lay on the sliced sausage.

7. And bake until the edges are golden and the cheese is melted, 10 to 12 minutes.

2. Slice the focaccia loaf in half crosswise.

5. Sprinkle on the artichoke hearts and kalamata olives.

8. Sprinkle with the Parmesan, then add dabs of pesto. Garnish with fresh basil and serve.

Almost everything's from the pantry!

Peach and Prosciutto Flatbread

MAKES 2 SERVINGS

The beauty of pizza is that if you don't want to fiddle with fresh dough, you can make it with any kind of flatbread you find in the supermarket! Pita bread, lavash, even tortillas can pass as a pizza crust—but my favorite has to be naan, which is soft but also crisps up around the edges when baked. I love it, and this prosciutto-peach version is probably my favorite of all time. (At least today.)

2 tablespoons olive oil

2 garlic cloves, minced

1 tablespoon minced fresh rosemary

2 naan flatbreads

4 ounces thinly sliced prosciutto

2 ounces crumbled goat cheese

¼ cup peach preserves

1½ cups baby arugula

Balsamic glaze

1. Preheat the oven to 375°F.

2. In a small bowl, mix the olive oil, garlic, and rosemary.

4. Add the prosciutto in bundles and top with the crumbled goat cheese.

6. Pile on the arugula . . .

3. Set the flatbreads on a sheet pan and brush the mixture all over the surface of the breads, making sure to coat the edges as well.

5. Bake the flatbreads until lightly toasted, about 10 minutes. Remove from the oven and add small spoonfuls of the preserves.

7. And drizzle on some balsamic glaze in a crisscross pattern.

8. Transfer to a cutting board and slice!

Salty, sweet, and ready in 15 minutes!

Turkey

Grilled in the waffle maker!

Reuben

Wafflewiches

MAKES 4 GENEROUS WAFFLE SANDWICHES

Wafflewiches are sandwiches made in waffle irons, and they're all kinds of brilliant. If you don't have a dedicated panini press, this is the next best way to make pressed-and-grilled sandwiches, and the little crevices on the surface of the bread add up to crispy, flavorful yumminess. To make it more DIY for your family, just lay out the breads, spreads, and fillings and let them assemble their own. Plus, it's just really, really fun to say "Wafflewiches!" (Try it. You'll see.)

Here are two of my favorite varieties, but making up your own is part of the experience.

TURKEY-BACON WAFFLEWICHES

4 slices wheat bread

⅓ cup Dijon mustard

4 slices cheddar cheese

8 thin slices deli turkey

½ cup baby spinach

½ small red onion, thinly sliced

8 slices bacon, cooked to crisp and broken in half

4 tablespoons (½ stick) salted butter, at room temperature

REUBEN WAFFLEWICHES

4 slices pumpernickel rye bread

⅓ cup Thousand Island dressing

4 slices Swiss cheese

8 slices pastrami

½ cup sauerkraut, drained

4 tablespoons (½ stick) salted butter, at room temperature

1. Preheat a waffle iron to low to medium-low heat.

2. Make the turkey-bacon wafflewiches: Spread the mustard on all 4 bread slices.

4. Then lay the turkey on 2 of the slices. Fold the turkey over or bundle it up, whatever works!

3. Lay a slice of cheddar on each slice of bread . . .

5. Next up: the spinach and red onion over the turkey . . .

6. Followed by the bacon. Go big or go home!

9. Add a slice of Swiss to each slice of bread, then add the pastrami to 2 of the slices.

13. Place all 4 sandwiches butter side down in the waffle iron. Spread the remaining butter on the top sides . . .

7. Bring the halves together to make 2 sandwiches, then set aside.

10. Pile the sauerkraut on top of the pastrami . . .

14. And close the waffle iron. Let them cook until the bread is golden and all the cheeses are melted, 4 to 5 minutes.

8. Make the Reuben wafflewiches: Spread the Thousand Island dressing on all 4 slices of pumpernickel rye.

11. Then bring the halves together to form two Reubens!

15. Carefully lift them out of the waffle iron with a fork or spatula.

12. Spread softened butter on the top side of all 4 sandwiches.

16. Transfer to a cutting board and slice them in half!

Four Seasons Pizza

MAKES ONE 12-INCH PIZZA

This is a very elegant pizza served on a decidedly *non*elegant crust. To be ultraspecific, the pizza crust shown in these photos is one of those prebaked supermarket stars that're sold in a value three-pack. That just goes to show you that convenience ingredients need to be embraced, baby!

This pizza is glorious, colorful . . . oh, and did I mention fast, easy, and fun?

PIZZA SAUCE

½ cup tomato puree

1 tablespoon dried oregano

½ teaspoon kosher salt

¼ teaspoon black pepper

1 tablespoon olive oil

PIZZA

1 tablespoon olive oil

3 ounces cremini mushrooms, sliced

Kosher salt and black pepper

One 12-inch store-bought pizza crust

1½ cups grated mozzarella cheese

3 marinated artichoke hearts, drained and quartered

3 tablespoons grated Fontina cheese

10 to 12 pepperoni slices

4 kalamata olives, pitted and halved lengthwise

2 ounces fresh mozzarella cheese, cut into cubes

8 cherry tomatoes, halved

2 tablespoons freshly grated Parmesan cheese, for garnish

4 fresh basil leaves, torn, for garnish

1. Preheat the oven to 450°F.

2. First, make the pizza sauce (or save time by using store-bought!): In a medium bowl, combine the tomato puree, oregano, salt, pepper, olive oil, and 1 tablespoon water . . .

3. And stir to combine. Set aside. It will keep in the fridge for several days if you want to make it ahead!

4. Next, start the pizza: In a 12-inch ovenproof skillet, heat the olive oil over medium-high heat. Add the mushrooms, sprinkle with salt and pepper to taste, and cook, stirring often, until golden, about 5 minutes. Remove them to a bowl and turn off the heat.

5. Lay the pizza crust in the same skillet . . .

Un-fancy store-bought crust!

6. Add 2 to 3 tablespoons of the pizza sauce and spread it all over the pizza, going up to but not over the rim.

9. To another quarter, add the artichoke hearts and Fontina. I changed my mind; this section's my favorite.

12. Bake the pizza until the crust is crisp and the cheese is all melted, about 10 minutes.

7. Cover the sauce with the mozzarella. Now it's time to build the four seasons!

10. Add the pepperoni and kalamata olives to the third quarter. (The third fourth. Ha.)

13. Sprinkle on Parmesan and torn fresh basil and serve to the pizza lovers in your life!

8. Add the mushrooms to one-quarter of the pizza. I think this section's my favorite.

11. And finally, add the mozzarella and tomatoes to the final section.

VARIATIONS

» *Use store-bought pizza dough, naan bread, frozen bread dough, or any easy pizza crust you like!*

» *Sub in any of your favorite pizza toppings and cheeses.*

OTHER PIZZA THEMES

The Devil's Playground: spicy arrabbiata sauce, fresh mozzarella, jarred spicy sliced peppers, crushed red pepper flakes. Nice and dangerous!

I'm a Funghi: wine-garlic sautéed mushrooms, grated Fontina, fresh oregano leaves, fresh ground black pepper. A mushroom paradise!

BLT: Alfredo sauce, grated cheddar-Jack, chopped cooked bacon. After baking, top with shredded lettuce, diced tomatoes, and a sprinkle of black pepper.

Pick a Pepper: grated mozzarella, grated Asiago, sliced jarred roasted red peppers, sliced mini sweet peppers, fresh basil, grated Parmesan.

The crust is frozen bread dough!

Barbecue Chicken Pizza

MAKES 6 TO 8 SERVINGS

This is one of five recipes using frozen bread dough in this cookbook, but I could fill an entire cookbook with the ways I've used it through the years. The only complicated thing about using frozen dough is remembering to move it to the fridge to thaw out the day before (or, if you're thawing on the counter, 4 hours before). But if you can master that, you can make any pizza in the universe and be assured that you'll wind up with a delicious crust that tastes pretty darned homemade!

You will absolutely love this barbecue chicken pizza. It's saucy and a little spicy and so easy it should be a crime.

One 1-pound loaf frozen bread dough, thawed

3 tablespoons olive oil

⅔ cup barbecue sauce

2 cups grated provolone or mozzarella cheese

2 cups shredded cooked chicken (see page xxi)

1 small red onion, thinly sliced

½ cup jarred pickled jalapeño slices

Fresh cilantro leaves, for garnish

1. Preheat the oven to 425°F.

2. Flatten the dough and stretch it into a large oval on an ungreased sheet pan. Using a fork, prick the dough all over to keep it from puffing up while baking.

3. Generously brush the surface with some of the olive oil.

4. Brush on ⅓ cup of the barbecue sauce, leaving a 1-inch border all around . . .

5. Then sprinkle on the provolone.

6. In a bowl, toss the chicken with the remaining ⅓ cup barbecue sauce . . .

7. And arrange it all over the pizza . . .

8. Then add the red onion and jalapeño slices.

9. Brush the rim of the dough with the remaining olive oil and transfer to the oven.

10. Bake the pizza until the edges are golden and crisp, 15 to 17 minutes.

11. Garnish with cilantro leaves, then slice and dive in!

Paige loves the cowgirl life!

Cheeseburger Pizza

MAKES 8 SERVINGS

There is nothing traditionally "pizza" about this cheeseburger pizza, but that doesn't mean it isn't ridiculously delicious! It's got big cheeseburger flavor, right down to the toppings and the sesame seed "bun" crust all around the edge. It's a conversation starter and an easy supper, all at the same time!

Olive oil

1 pound ground beef

1 small onion, finely diced

Kosher salt and black pepper

¼ cup ketchup, plus more for drizzling

¼ cup yellow mustard, plus more for drizzling

1 teaspoon seasoned salt (such as Lawry's)

2 or 3 dashes of Worcestershire sauce

One 1-pound loaf frozen bread dough, thawed

2 cups grated cheddar cheese

1 cup grated mozzarella cheese

1 tablespoon sesame seeds

2 cups finely shredded lettuce

2 Roma tomatoes, diced

1 cup finely diced pickles

3 slices bacon, cooked to crisp and roughly chopped

Sliced green onions, for garnish

1. In a medium skillet, heat a little olive oil over medium-high heat. Add the ground beef, onion, and a pinch each of salt and pepper. Cook until the meat is browned. Pour off any excess grease.

2. Add the ketchup, mustard, seasoned salt, and Worcestershire . . .

3. And stir to coat the meat. Cook for another couple of minutes, then remove it from the heat.

4. Stretch the dough into a large oval on an ungreased sheet pan.

5. Drizzle with a little olive oil and sprinkle with salt and pepper.

6. Mix the two cheeses together and sprinkle two-thirds of the mixture over the dough, leaving a 1-inch border all around.

7. Spoon on the meat mixture . . .

8. Then add the rest of the cheese, reserving a tiny bit for garnish.

9. Brush the edges of the crust with olive oil . . .

10. Then sprinkle on the sesame seeds.

11. Bake the pizza until the cheese is melted and the crust is golden, 15 to 17 minutes.

12. (This is optional!) Drizzle a little ketchup and mustard back and forth over the top.

13. Top the pizza with the lettuce and tomatoes . . .

14. And sprinkle with the pickles, bacon, and green onions. Delicious cheeseburger goodness!

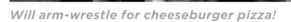

Will arm-wrestle for cheeseburger pizza!

Frozen bread dough!

PASTA AND GRAINS

And speaking of carbs . . . can we talk about pasta for a minute? *Pasta, pasta, pasta, pasta, pasta.* Okay, great talk! Pasta is my love language, and it has been since I was about a year old, when my mom first fed me mac and cheese. Thus began a lifelong love affair with noodles, and to me, they've never gone out of style. Aside from pasta's obvious appeal, I think it's had such staying power in my kitchen because it's the basis of so many incredibly easy dinners, which I've needed in abundance through the years. This list of pasta (and grain) recipes will awaken the noodle lover in you. I apologize in advance for all of this deliciousness!

A new family favorite!

Taco Shells and Cheese

MAKES 6 TO 8 SERVINGS

This is a crazy-quick, ultra-satisfying spin on mac and cheese, and the fanciest thing about it is . . . well, I can't think of anything fancy about it! I tried. It's an incredible combination of fridge and pantry staples, which is why I find myself making it at least a couple of times a month in my house—especially during the school year, when "busy" doesn't even begin to describe our wonderfully wacky days. Feel free to bump up the spice, and definitely feel free to add, remove, or sub any of the ingredients. Use different cheeses, leave it meatless, add sautéed veggies, or use ground turkey. There are no right or wrong answers!

2 tablespoons olive oil

4 tablespoons (½ stick) salted butter

1 pound ground beef

Kosher salt and black pepper

2 teaspoons chili powder

1 teaspoon ground cumin

1 teaspoon onion powder

½ teaspoon garlic powder

½ teaspoon paprika

One 10-ounce can Ro*tel (diced tomatoes and green chilies)

2 cups whole milk, or more as needed

8 ounces processed cheese (such as Velveeta), diced

2½ cups freshly grated cheddar-Jack cheese (or any combo of cheddar and Jack)

1 pound small pasta shells, cooked according to the package directions and drained

¼ cup chopped fresh cilantro, plus more for serving

Sour cream and jarred salsa (optional), for serving

1. In a large skillet, heat the olive oil and 2 tablespoons of the butter over medium-high heat. Add the ground beef and cook until browned, crumbling it with a spoon or spatula.

2. Add the chili powder, cumin, onion powder, garlic powder, and paprika and stir to combine.

3. Add the Ro*tel and 1 cup hot water . . .

4. And stir and cook for 3 minutes to let the sauce thicken slightly.

5. Pour the meat mixture into a heatproof bowl and set aside.

6. Return the pan (do not clean the pan!) to the stove over medium heat. Add the remaining 2 tablespoons butter, the milk, and a pinch of salt and pepper . . .

7. And stir until the butter and milk mixture is hot. Add the Velveeta and stir. Things are getting interesting!

8. Add the cheddar-Jack and stir to melt. Turn off the heat.

9. Add the cooked pasta and the meat mixture . . .

10. And stir this glorious yumminess until everything is well combined.

11. Add the cilantro and stir!

12. Serve piping hot garnished with extra cilantro. If you want, top with a spoonful of salsa and sour cream!

VARIATIONS

» *Add diced fresh jalapeño for another layer of heat.*

» *Add several dashes of hot sauce for a little tang.*

Sheet Pan Gnocchi

MAKES 6 SERVINGS

Packaged gnocchi are one of my most favorite ingredients during this need-things-to-be-easier season in my life. Does that make me sound old? Good, because I meant for it to!

All self-deprecating old lady references aside, this meatless marvel is both a cinch and a revelation: soft and tender gnocchi pillows roasted on a sheet pan with the best variety of veggies and topped with Parmesan and basil. Give me this, a clear to-do list, a glass of wine . . . and I'm just fine.

¼ cup olive oil

¼ cup prepared pesto

One 16-ounce package gnocchi

1 pound asparagus, ends trimmed, cut into 1-inch pieces

1 red onion, cut into large chunks

1 orange bell pepper, thinly sliced

1 yellow bell pepper, thinly sliced

Kosher salt and black pepper

1 cup mixed yellow and red cherry tomatoes

2 tablespoons balsamic glaze

Freshly shaved Parmesan cheese, for serving

¼ cup fresh basil leaves

1. Preheat the oven to 450°F.

2. In a small pitcher or bowl, mix together the olive oil and pesto.

4. And toss everything to coat. Sprinkle with salt and black pepper and roast for 10 minutes.

6. Sprinkle the tomatoes on top and toss. Return to the oven until the edges of the gnocchi have begun to get golden and crisp, about 10 minutes.

3. Lay the gnocchi, asparagus, onion, and bell peppers on a sheet pan. Pour the pesto-oil mixture over everything . . .

5. Remove the pan from the oven and toss again.

7. Give the mix one final toss . . .

8. And serve in bowls. Garnish with the balsamic glaze . . .

9. And Parmesan shavings and basil!

VARIATIONS

» *Add peeled raw shrimp to the pan with the veggies for a bit of seafood!*

» *Sub in or add any veggies you like: halved mushrooms, zucchini chunks, fresh green beans, and so forth.*

The squad!

Store-bought gnocchi makes it easy!

The Best Fettuccine Alfredo

MAKES 4 TO 6 SERVINGS

It isn't hard to get fettuccine Alfredo right. I mean, how could butter, garlic, cream, Parmesan, and pasta ever go south? Still, I have found that the timing and the order of ingredients can help up the perfection factor even more. Here's how I love to make mine—on the two occasions per year I allow myself to eat it. My gosh, this is rich!

½ cup (1 stick) salted butter

5 garlic cloves, peeled

2 cups heavy cream

2 cups freshly grated Parmesan cheese

Kosher salt and black pepper

12 ounces fettuccine, cooked according to the package directions and drained

Grated zest of 2 lemons, for serving

Minced fresh parsley, for serving

1. In a large skillet, melt the butter over medium heat. Press the garlic through a press into the butter . . .

3. Pour in the cream . . .

5. Add the Parmesan . . .

2. And cook, stirring, for 2 minutes to allow the flavors to be released. (Smells so good!)

4. And stir, letting the mixture heat until it bubbles around the edges, about 5 minutes.

6. And stir until completely melted and smooth.

Super-fast Alfredo!

7. Add a small pinch of salt and as much pepper as you'd like! Stir to combine.

8. Add the drained pasta immediately to the sauce . . .

9. Toss the pasta with tongs until it's coated with sauce!

10. Pile in bowls and sprinkle on the lemon zest and parsley.

Life with Paige is fun!

One-Pot Sausage Pasta

MAKES 6 TO 8 SERVINGS

All pasta is inherently good. This age-old truth is written on my heart, and I doubt it will ever change. But this dish, which is made all in one pot without cooking the pasta separately, has ascended to the top of my list of favorite pastas for two significant reasons: One, it's so darn easy. And two, it's so incredibly delicious. Never a noodle left!

1 tablespoon olive oil

1 pound sweet Italian sausage, casings removed

1 yellow onion, diced

2 teaspoons dried oregano

½ teaspoon fennel seeds

Pinch of red pepper flakes

2 garlic cloves, minced

Kosher salt and black pepper

One 28-ounce can tomato puree

2 tablespoons tomato paste

4 cups (1 quart) low-sodium chicken broth

1 pound fusilli pasta

⅓ cup mascarpone cheese

1½ cups grated mozzarella cheese

¼ cup Parmesan shavings, plus more for serving

10 to 12 fresh basil leaves, plus more for serving

1. In a large deep skillet, heat the olive oil over medium heat. Add the sausage and cook and crumble it until it starts to brown, about 5 minutes.

3. Add the oregano, fennel seeds, red pepper flakes, garlic, and salt and black pepper to taste. Stir to combine.

5. The tomato paste . . .

2. Add the onion and cook, stirring often, until softened and translucent and the sausage is well browned, 5 to 7 minutes.

4. Add the tomato puree . . .

6. And the broth . . .

7. And stir to make sure everything is well combined.

8. Dump in the pasta right out of the package . . .

9. And stir until it's totally coated in sauce.

10. Turn the heat to low and put the lid on the pan.

11. Simmer, stirring occasionally, until the pasta has absorbed the liquid and is tender, about 20 minutes.

12. Turn off the heat. Add the mascarpone and stir to combine.

13. Add the mozzarella . . .

14. And stir until it's melted.

15. Add the Parmesan shavings and the basil, tearing the larger leaves as you add them.

Garnish with more Parmesan shavings and basil and serve right out of the pan!

VEGGIE VERSION

For a lighter version of the one-pot pasta, sauté 1 diced onion and 3 minced garlic cloves in a little olive oil. Add 1 cup white wine and 4 cups (1 quart) vegetable stock and stir to combine. Add the uncooked pasta, 1 bunch chopped Broccolini, 2 sliced carrots, and 2 cups cauliflower florets. Cover and cook for 20 minutes, until the pasta is almost done. Stir in 1 cup heavy cream, 1 cup grated Parmesan, and 2 tablespoons pesto. Yum!

No pre-cooking the pasta!

Ree's Favorite Noodles

MAKES 6 SERVINGS

I'm obsessed with this noodle dish, and you will be, too! It's based on my well-loved (by me, at least!) sesame noodle recipe, which is a perfect side dish, main dish, or snack. This version brings in mushrooms, which soak up the flavorful sauce and give the noodles an added layer of texture and flavor that'll make you go *Mmmmmm*. Like, totally.

Super-duper fast!

4 tablespoons (½ stick) salted butter

8 ounces cremini mushrooms, thinly sliced

4 ounces shiitake mushroom caps, thinly sliced

4 ounces oyster mushrooms, torn

¼ cup soy sauce

¼ cup vegetable oil

3 tablespoons toasted sesame oil

2 tablespoons rice vinegar

½ teaspoon hot chile oil

2 tablespoons sugar

4 garlic cloves, minced

8 ounces thin spaghetti, cooked according to the package directions and drained

4 green onions, thinly sliced

1. In a large skillet, melt the butter over medium-high heat. Add the mushrooms . . .

4. Stir with a fork to combine . . .

8. Add most of the green onions . . .

2. And cook until tender and golden brown, about 5 minutes.

5. And pour the sauce over the mushrooms. Stir and cook the mushrooms in the sauce until hot and bubbling, about 2 minutes.

9. And toss everything together, allowing the noodles to absorb the rest of the sauce. Serve with green onions sprinkled over the top.

3. While the mushrooms are cooking, in a small pitcher or bowl, combine the soy sauce, vegetable oil, sesame oil, vinegar, chile oil, sugar, and garlic.

6. Turn off the heat, add the spaghetti . . .

7. And toss them with the mushrooms.

VARIATIONS

» *Use any combination of mushrooms you'd like!*

» *Add a splash of sherry to the sauce for a little added magic.*

» *Add diced hot chile peppers to the pan with the mushrooms for a spicier dish.*

» *Add sliced red and green bell peppers to the pan with the mushrooms for some added color and flavor.*

» *Serve sliced grilled steak or chicken over the noodles.*

Sheet Pan Mac and Cheese

MAKES 8 TO 10 SERVINGS

If you're the kind of person who gets their jollies by eating the baked cheese topping off of a mac and cheese casserole, this recipe is going to make your day. By baking the mac and cheese in a sheet pan instead of the typical deep casserole dish, you ensure a lot more surface area to fulfill all your baked cheese dreams! And to drive home the crispy cheesy edges, I like to heat the sheet pan before the mac and cheese gets poured in. The sizzle is the key!

Three words: *Come to Mama.*

Two 12-ounce cans evaporated milk

8 ounces processed cheese (such as Velveeta), cut into large cubes

3 cups grated cheddar cheese

2 cups grated Gruyère cheese

1 teaspoon hot sauce

1 teaspoon dry mustard

Kosher salt and black pepper

1 pound elbow macaroni, cooked 1 minute less than on the package directions and drained

Cooking spray

1 cup grated Parmesan cheese

Chopped fresh parsley, for garnish

1. Preheat the oven to 425°F.

2. Place a sheet pan in the oven to heat while you make the mac and cheese.

4. Whisk in the Velveeta, melting it halfway.

6. The mustard and salt and pepper to taste.

3. Pour the evaporated milk into a large skillet. Set over medium heat and bring it to a simmer, stirring.

5. Add 1½ cups of the cheddar, 1 cup of the Gruyère, the hot sauce . . .

7. Continue whisking until the cheeses are totally melted and the sauce is smooth.

Lots of tasty surface area!

8. Add the macaroni and stir to coat, then taste, adjust the seasonings, and turn off the heat.

10. Pour in the macaroni, scraping in all the sauce, and smooth it into an even layer.

9. Remove the sheet pan from the oven and immediately mist it with cooking spray.

11. In a medium bowl, mix the remaining 1½ cups cheddar, remaining 1 cup Gruyère, and the Parmesan. Sprinkle the cheeses over the macaroni.

12. Bake until the cheese is bubbling and golden, 18 to 20 minutes. Serve with a sprinkle of parsley.

Even an old truck can dress up for a wedding!

Hawaiian Shrimp Bowls

MAKES 4 SERVINGS

I love a big ol' bowl of food! Especially when it's brimming with beautiful colors and textures and flavors, and *especially* when it's cooked with easy bottled sauce and served on microwavable rice. It just makes me feel happy. And hopeful. And lazy! (In a good way, of course.)

¾ cup teriyaki sauce

2 tablespoons Thai sweet chili sauce

1 tablespoon olive oil, plus more for the grill pan

4 thick slices fresh pineapple (buy it already prepped in the produce section!)

1 pound extra jumbo shrimp (16/20 count), peeled and deveined

12 mini sweet peppers

One 8.5-ounce package microwave jasmine rice, or any rice, heated according to package directions

2 avocados, diced

2 limes, cut into wedges

1 tablespoon toasted sesame seeds

1 cup fresh cilantro leaves

1. Preheat a grill pan over medium heat.

2. Pour the teriyaki sauce, sweet chili sauce, and olive oil into a bowl . . .

3. And stir to combine.

4. Brush some olive oil onto the grill pan, then lay on the pineapple and some of the shrimp and peppers.

5. Brush the veggies and shrimp with the sauce and let them cook for a couple of minutes.

6. When everything has great color and grill marks, turn it over to the other side . . .

7. And generously brush with more of the sauce. Let cook for 1½ minutes, then turn them over to the first side again to heat the sauce thoroughly and caramelize a bit (the shrimp is fully cooked when it's opaque). Remove to a plate, then repeat with the rest of the shrimp and peppers.

Microwave rice!
And I ain't sorry!

8. Proudly dump a helping of microwave rice in a bowl . . .

10. Add some of the avocado and some lime wedges . . .

11. Then add a sprinkle of sesame seeds and some cilantro leaves. So pretty and appealing!

9. Then arrange some peppers, pineapple (I cut a slice in half), and shrimp over the rice.

VARIATIONS

» *Substitute thin chicken cutlets for the shrimp. Slice the chicken after grilling.*

» *Serve everything over green leaf lettuce instead of rice for a lovely salad.*

» *Substitute slabs of bell pepper for the mini peppers.*

Makeshift TV crew!

Risotto without
the stirring!

Baked Risotto

MAKES 8 TO 10 SERVINGS

I've loved risotto all my life. Just kidding, I've loved it since about 1990, when I went out to dinner with a California co-worker who ordered it for me and told me, quite correctly, that I was about to fall in love. (With the risotto, not the co-worker.)

Thirty (what??) years later, I still love risotto and while I'm fine to make it the traditional way—i.e., standing at the stove for upward of 45 minutes, adding broth and stirring constantly—this oven method is a total gift and game changer for me. So while it isn't necessarily faster than the original, it does free you up to live your life (or get the rest of dinner ready, or nap) while it's cooking in the oven.

Use this same formula for whatever your favorite risotto variation is. Works every time!

2 tablespoons salted butter

½ medium onion, finely diced

2 garlic cloves, minced

8 ounces cremini mushrooms, sliced

1 tablespoon chopped fresh rosemary leaves

1 tablespoon fresh thyme leaves

1 teaspoon kosher salt

½ teaspoon black pepper

1½ cups Arborio rice

½ cup white wine (such as Sauvignon Blanc) or low-sodium vegetable broth

6 cups low-sodium vegetable broth, plus more as needed

4 cups chopped stemmed kale

1 cup grated Fontina or Monterey Jack cheese

2 tablespoons chopped fresh parsley, plus more for garnish

Juice of 1 lemon

Lemon wedges, for serving

1. Preheat the oven to 400°F.

2. In an ovenproof skillet with a tight-fitting lid, heat the butter over medium-high heat. Add the onion, garlic, and mushrooms . . .

3. And cook, stirring, for about 10 minutes . . .

4. Until the onions are deep golden brown. Add the herbs, salt, and pepper . . .

5. And mix them in.

6. Add the rice and stir to coat it with the sauce, cooking for 1 minute.

7. Then comes the wine, which is mighty fine. (Actually it's mighty cheap. Any ol' white wine will do!)

8. Stir and let the rice start to absorb the wine . . .

9. Then add the broth and stir well.

10. Add the kale and mix it in.

11. Put the lid on the pan and bake in the oven (without stirring!) for 50 minutes.

12. Carefully remove the lid. (It will be very steamy inside!) Add the Fontina, parsley, and lemon juice . . .

13. And stir to combine! If it seems dry at all, stir in up to 1 cup additional warm broth.

14. Sprinkle on extra parsley and serve with lemon wedges.

OTHER RISOTTO IDEAS

You can use the same method of cooking onions and garlic in butter and adding arborio rice, wine, and broth to make any kind of risotto under the sun! Here are three delicious variations:

Classic: Omit vegetables altogether and just cook the wine, broth, and rice with the onion, garlic, and butter. When it's done, stir in 1½ cups grated Parmesan cheese and garnish with parsley.

Caprese: Make the classic version above, and when done, stir in 2 cups halved grape tomatoes, chunks of fresh mozzarella cheese, and 3 tablespoons pesto. Garnish with Parmesan shavings and balsamic glaze.

Primavera: Add asparagus, chunks of zucchini, sliced mushrooms, and chunks of yellow squash. Use vegetable stock, and when the risotto is done, stir in thawed frozen peas, heavy cream, ricotta, and Parmesan cheese. Garnish with fresh basil.

Broccoli-Cheese Orzotto

MAKES 6 TO 8 SERVINGS

Orzotto is a cross between pasta and risotto, and it's an absolute miracle. Instead of using Arborio rice that you'd normally use to make risotto, you use orzo pasta, which cooks in a fraction of the time. I created this broccoli-cheese spin sometime in the past couple of years, and it is absolutely out of this world! Just ask the Drummond kids. They're fans.

2 tablespoons salted butter

½ yellow onion, finely diced

1 garlic clove, grated

2 cups orzo pasta

6 cups (1½ quarts) vegetable or chicken broth, warmed

1 teaspoon dry mustard

½ teaspoon cayenne pepper

½ teaspoon kosher salt, plus more to taste

½ teaspoon black pepper, plus more to taste

2 pounds broccoli florets (can use frozen)

One 4-ounce jar pimientos, undrained

8 ounces Velveeta, cut into cubes

1½ cups grated cheddar cheese

Chopped fresh parsley, for garnish

1. In a large skillet, melt the butter over medium-high heat. Add the onion and garlic and cook, stirring often, until the onion starts to soften, about 2 minutes.

2. Add the orzo and stir to coat. Cook for another minute, stirring constantly.

3. Use a ladle to add 2 cups of the broth . . .

4. And stir until the liquid starts to be absorbed by the orzo.

5. Add the dry mustard, cayenne, salt, and black pepper . . .

6. And stir until all the liquid is absorbed.

Orzo pasta cooked like risotto!

7. Add 2 more cups of the broth and cook, stirring often, until it's absorbed . . .

9. Add the broccoli and pimientos . . .

11. Add the Velveeta and stir until it's melted, about 1 minute.

8. Then add the rest of the broth!

10. And bring to a gentle boil. Cook, stirring occasionally, until the orzo is cooked, about 6 more minutes.

12. Finally, add the cheddar . . .

13. And stir it until it's melted and the sauce is creamy. Taste and add more salt and pepper as needed. Serve with a sprinkle of parsley.

Strange bedfellows!

- -

VARIATIONS

» *Substitute cauliflower florets for half the broccoli.*

» *Substitute pepper Jack for the cheddar.*

» *Add a spoonful of pesto with the cheeses.*

» *Add finely diced chicken breast with the onions and garlic for a meatier dish.*

Very Green Orzotto

MAKES 8 TO 10 SERVINGS

I love all the recipes in this cookbook or they wouldn't have made the cut, but at the risk of hurting their feelings, I have to state that I think I love this recipe a little more! Creamy orzo cooked like risotto, with every green vegetable and herb I can get my hands on . . . my goodness gracious, it's incredible! I could eat it morning, noon, and night for eighty years straight. Maybe even eighty-one!

2 tablespoons olive oil

4 green onions, thinly sliced

2 garlic cloves, minced

¼ teaspoon red pepper flakes

2 cups orzo pasta

Kosher salt and black pepper

6 cups (1½ quarts) low-sodium vegetable broth, warmed

½ pound asparagus, ends trimmed, cut into 2-inch pieces

½ bunch Broccolini, ends trimmed, cut into 2-inch pieces

1 cup frozen green peas

2 medium zucchini, quartered lengthwise and cut crosswise into 2-inch batons

½ cup shredded kale (stems and ribs removed)

½ cup freshly grated Parmesan cheese, plus more for garnish

Grated zest of 1 lemon

¼ cup chopped fresh basil, plus more for garnish

¼ cup chopped fresh flat-leaf parsley, plus more for garnish

1. In a saucepan, heat the oil over medium heat. Add the green onions, garlic, and red pepper flakes . . .

3. Pour in the orzo . . .

5. Reduce the heat to medium. Ladle in 2 cups of the warmed broth, stir gently, and bring to a boil.

2. And stir and cook for about 30 seconds, until fragrant.

4. And stir to coat it in the oil and green onion mixture.

6. Cook, stirring, until most of the liquid is absorbed, 2 to 3 minutes. Just like risotto!

My favorite!
Green and gorgeous.

7. Add 2 more cups of the broth. Cook, stirring, until this, too, has been absorbed, another 2 to 3 minutes.

9. Add the zucchini . . .

11. When the liquid is almost totally absorbed, add the kale, Parmesan, lemon zest, basil, and parsley . . .

8. Add the remaining 2 cups broth along with the asparagus, Broccolini, and peas.

10. And cook the mixture for another 2 to 3 minutes, stirring often.

12. And cook, stirring, for another 2 minutes. Turn off the heat; the broth will continue to be absorbed by the orzo! Serve with more Parmesan, basil, and parsley.

A few good men!

Ravioli alla Betsy

MAKES 6 TO 8 SERVINGS

My younger sister Betsy is a great cook, and her Penne alla Betsy pasta dish is one of my favorite recipes of all time. I love it so much, in fact, that I put it in my very first cookbook so many years ago . . . and I still love it so much that I knew I had to include this variation in my new cookbook. Seven cookbooks from now, I will probably include yet another variation because, well, the foundational recipe is really that good.

This recipe comes together in less than 20 minutes, which is a triumph. And just wait till you take your first bite.

4 tablespoons (½ stick) salted butter

2 tablespoons olive oil

1 pound peeled deveined large shrimp

Kosher salt and black pepper

1 medium yellow onion, finely diced

3 garlic cloves, grated

⅔ cup white wine (or veggie stock)

Two 15-ounce cans tomato sauce

1 cup heavy cream

¼ cup chopped fresh flat-leaf parsley, plus more for garnish

8 fresh basil leaves, roughly chopped, plus more for garnish

18 to 20 ounces packaged spinach ravioli (fresh or frozen), cooked to just barely al dente according to the package directions

1. In a large skillet, melt 2 tablespoons of the butter with 1 tablespoon of the olive oil over medium-high heat. Add the shrimp, sprinkle with a pinch of salt and pepper . . .

2. And cook on the first side for about 1 minute. Flip the shrimp over and cook until opaque, another minute.

3. Remove the shrimp to a plate and set aside.

4. Add the remaining 2 tablespoons butter and 1 tablespoon olive oil to the pan, then sprinkle in the onion and garlic . . .

5. And cook, stirring often, until the onion is starting to soften, about 3 minutes.

6. Add the wine and scrape the bottom of the skillet to loosen up any bits. Cook the wine until reduced by about half, about 2 minutes.

7. Add the tomato sauce and stir for 1 minute to heat through.

11. Add the shrimp to the sauce and stir.

13. When the sauce comes to a gentle boil, add the cooked ravioli.

8. Add the cream and season with pepper to taste . . .

12. Add the parsley and basil and stir them into the sauce. Things are getting exciting!

14. Gently toss the ravioli until it's totally coated with sauce. I want to cry, this is so amazing!

Serve it with a sprinkle of herbs on top.

9. And stir until the sauce turns a beautiful salmon pink! Reduce the heat to medium-low.

10. Transfer the shrimp to a cutting board and chop them into large bite-size pieces.

JAMAR

The graduate!

My sister's specialty!

EASY SKILLETS

When it comes to everyday cooking, there's nothing I use more often than a skillet. From cast iron to stainless to anodized to nonstick, I've got a multicolored mishmash of them at my fingertips at all times. I love the kind of dinners that can be made in a skillet, especially those that don't dirty up a bunch of other pots and bowls, and that's exactly what this list of recipes delivers. You'll find lots of protein and flavor variety here, and most of these are perfect for both weeknight family meals and weekend suppers with buddies. And to stir things up a little bit, I've thrown in a handful of my favorite sides for some of these dishes. You'll love 'em all!

Coated in cornflake crumbs!

Chicken-Fried Steak Fingers

MAKES 3 OR 4 SERVINGS

There is nothing on earth that says "I love you" to my family more than a dinner of chicken-fried steak. The only problem is that it's a total mess to make, which I find myself having less and less tolerance for as time goes on. Does that mean I'm getting old or lazy? Or both? Never mind! Don't answer that.

When I set out to make chicken-fried steak easier and more pain-free, I decided that the breading was usually the thing I dreaded the most. So for these easy-to-eat steak fingers, I swapped the heavy flour-milk-egg dunking process for a simple two-stage (and two-ingredient) substitute. I'm hooked. If chicken-fried steak is important to you and your'n, you're gonna want to pay attention to this.

STEAK FINGERS

1¼ pounds cube steak, cut into 1½-inch-thick strips

Kosher salt and black pepper

1 cup whole milk

1½ cups packaged cornflake crumbs

¼ cup canola oil, for frying

4 tablespoons (½ stick) salted butter, for frying, plus more as needed

Awesome Roasted Tomatoes (page 207), for serving

GRAVY

3 tablespoons all-purpose flour, plus more as needed

3 cups whole milk, plus more as needed

Pinch of kosher salt

Lots of black pepper

1. Make the steak fingers: Season the steak strips on both sides with salt and pepper.

3. And then immediately coat in the cornflake crumbs, pressing to get them as coated as possible!

5. In a large nonstick skillet, heat the oil and butter over medium heat. Add the steak fingers and cook them until golden brown on one side, about 2 minutes . . .

2. One at a time, dunk them in the milk . . .

4. Keep going until you've breaded all the meat, then set aside on a plate.

6. Then flip them over and cook until browned on the other side, 1½ to 2 minutes.

7. Place them on a plate lined with paper towels and set aside while you make the gravy!

8. Set the same skillet back on the stove. Sprinkle the flour over the grease and drippings in the skillet . . .

9. And whisk to mix it into a paste. If it's too dry, add another tablespoon of butter. If it's too greasy, sprinkle in a couple teaspoons of flour.

10. Cook, whisking constantly, until the roux is a deep golden brown.

11. Pour in the milk, whisking constantly until smooth.

12. Add the salt and pepper and continue to cook the gravy, whisking constantly . . .

13. Until it's thick enough to coat a spoon. If it gets too thick, you can thin it with a little milk! If it isn't thick enough, just keep cooking it. It'll get there!

14. Taste and adjust the seasonings. I like to have an extra steak finger on hand just for this!

15. Serve with gravy on the side. (Ketchup is yummy, too!) Serve with Awesome Roasted Tomatoes.

AWESOME ROASTED TOMATOES

MAKES 6 SERVINGS

I think roasted tomatoes are just magic. Whatever light caramelization and roastiness happens in the oven, I'm a believer, and I think they make the perfect side for a variety of dishes.

Leave these plain or top them with this simple herby sauce . . . or any sauce! They'll be your new go-to veggie side. Promise.

TOMATOES

6 Roma tomatoes, halved lengthwise

¼ cup olive oil

2 garlic cloves, finely chopped

¼ teaspoon red pepper flakes

Kosher salt and black pepper

HERB DRIZZLE

¼ cup fresh basil leaves

2 tablespoons fresh oregano leaves and tender stems

1 tablespoon capers

Juice of 1 lemon

Kosher salt and black pepper

¼ cup extra-virgin olive oil

FOR SERVING

Small fresh basil leaves, for garnish

Fresh oregano leaves, for garnish

1. Preheat the oven to 400°F.

2. Prepare the tomatoes: Lay the tomatoes cut side up on a sheet pan and drizzle them with the olive oil.

3. Sprinkle on the garlic, pepper flakes, and salt and black pepper to taste. Transfer to the oven and roast them until starting to turn brown on top, about 30 minutes.

4. While the tomatoes are roasting, make the herb drizzle: In a small food processor or blender, combine the basil, oregano, capers, lemon juice, and salt and pepper to taste.

5. With the machine running, blend the mixture while drizzling in the extra-virgin olive oil.

6. Drizzle the herb mixture all over the roasted tomatoes.

7. Serve warm or at room temperature on a plate, with small basil and oregano leaves for garnish.

VARIATION

» *Skip the homemade herb drizzle and use store-bought pesto instead for an even easier side dish.*

Beef Noodle Skillet

MAKES 4 TO 6 SERVINGS

I'm not going to beat around the bush: This is a homemade version of Hamburger Helper. The much-maligned, cook-with-hamburger-and-slap-on-a-plate box mix—which my whole family happens to adore, by the way, ahem—was my inspiration and my muse. I'll bet if Hamburger Helper were a person, they would immediately start crying from happiness over having just been called an inspiration and muse . . . probably for the first time in their life.

This is a one-pan dish you'll fall in love with!

2 tablespoons salted butter

1 medium yellow onion, finely diced

3 garlic cloves, minced

1 pound ground chuck (any ground beef is fine)

Kosher salt and black pepper

3 tablespoons tomato paste

12 ounces egg noodles (No Yolks brand egg noodles work best)

2 tablespoons grainy mustard

1½ teaspoons smoked paprika

2½ cups beef broth

A few dashes of Worcestershire sauce

⅓ cup sour cream

2 tablespoons heavy cream

2 tablespoons chopped fresh chives

1. In a large skillet, combine the butter, onion, garlic, and ground chuck. Cook over medium heat, stirring often, until the meat is browned, about 5 minutes.

3. And let the tomato paste cook for about a minute, stirring.

5. The mustard and smoked paprika . . .

2. Drain the excess grease (I leave a little for flavor!). Stir in the tomato paste . . .

4. Add the (uncooked!) noodles . . .

6. The beef broth and Worcestershire . . .

Better than the box!

7. And, finally, 1 cup hot water.

9. Add the sour cream and heavy cream . . .

11. Top everything with chives and serve it right from the skillet!

8. Stir, cover, and reduce the heat to low. Simmer, stirring occasionally, until the pasta is just about al dente and the sauce has thickened a bit, about 10 minutes.

10. Stir gently and cook for about 1 more minute, until the sauce is perfect and the noodles are cooked. Season with salt and pepper to taste.

VARIATIONS

» *Slice 6 mushrooms and add them to the skillet with the diced onions.*

» *Use Greek yogurt in place of the sour cream and heavy cream.*

» *Top with 3 sliced green onions instead of chives.*

Three brothers with a microphone . . . Be afraid! Be very afraid.

Stir-Fry with Scallops

MAKES 4 TO 6 SERVINGS

When it comes to building a nice, robust repertoire of fast and easy recipes, you'd better make sure you have plenty of stir-fry options. They're the absolute best: flavorful, colorful, and oh so fresh. I use this basic formula (and sauce) no matter what my proteins and veggies are, and it has never let me down!

Sub shrimp for the scallops if you'd prefer, or combine them to have the best of both worlds. I'm a fan of the mysterious scallop, so that'll always be my first choice!

½ cup reduced-sodium soy sauce

2 tablespoons rice vinegar

2 tablespoons packed brown sugar

1 tablespoon minced fresh ginger

1½ tablespoons cornstarch

About 2 teaspoons sriracha, or to taste

3 tablespoons peanut or vegetable oil

1 pound scallops (10 to 12), rinsed with cold water and patted dry with paper towels

1 head broccoli, cut into florets

1 yellow summer squash, cut into medium dice

One 15-ounce can baby corn, drained and halved lengthwise

8 ounces snow peas, trimmed

1 Fresno pepper, thinly sliced (you can also use jalapeño)

3 green onions, thinly sliced

Microwave jasmine or white rice, heated according to the package directions

¼ cup fresh cilantro leaves

1. Heat a large nonstick skillet over medium-high heat.

2. In a pitcher or spouted cup, combine the soy sauce, vinegar, brown sugar, ginger, cornstarch, and sriracha . . .

4. Add the peanut oil to the hot skillet, then add the scallops. Let them sear on one side for about 2 minutes . . .

3. And stir with a fork until well combined. Set aside.

5. Then flip them over to sear on the other side for about 1½ minutes. They are ready when they have just turned opaque.

6. Remove the scallops to a plate and set aside.

7. Crank up the heat under the skillet to high. Add the broccoli, squash, and baby corn and stir and cook for about 2 minutes . . .

8. Then add the snow peas and sliced pepper.

9. Stir and cook for another minute to soften the snow peas, then reduce the heat to low.

10. Give the sauce another stir, then pour it all over the veggies. It will start to bubble immediately!

11. Pour in ½ cup water . . .

12. And stir with a spatula, tossing the veggies to coat them in the sauce as you go. The sauce should be thick and glossy! If it's too thick, you can splash in a little more water.

13. When the veggies are saucy, add the scallops, making sure to include the flavorful juices from the plate.

14. Carefully toss everything together, being gentle with the scallops! You don't want to hurt their feelings.

15. Sprinkle on the green onions and serve over rice. Sprinkle cilantro leaves over the top.

. . . .

VARIATIONS

» *Substitute shrimp, chicken, or beef for the scallops. This formula works for a wide variety of stir-fry combinations.*

» *Keep it meatless and add more veggies, such as red bell pepper and mushrooms.*

» *Serve over noodles instead of rice, or eat on its own with no starch!*

Ready in 20 minutes!

Speedy Pork Scaloppine

MAKES 2 TO 4 SERVINGS

This is a light, pretty dinner for any night of the week, and is easy to pull together, whether it's for two people or more. I like to sub pork for the typical chicken in scaloppine, but it's really the lemony wine-caper sauce that's the star of the show. I could drink it with a straw!

PORK

4 thin-cut boneless pork chops

Kosher salt and black pepper

½ cup plus 2 tablespoons all-purpose flour

½ cup milk

1 large egg

⅔ cup Italian-style panko breadcrumbs

3 tablespoons olive oil

6 tablespoons (¾ stick) salted butter

2 tablespoons drained capers

⅔ cup white wine (or chicken broth)

⅓ cup chicken broth

Juice of ½ lemon

FOR SERVING

2 to 3 cups arugula

Lemon wedges

Freshly shaved Parmesan cheese

Freshly chopped fresh flat-leaf parsley

Loaded Crash Hots (page 218— you might want to double the recipe!)

1. Prepare the pork: One by one, place the pork chops between two pieces of plastic wrap and use a meat pounder or mallet to pound them very thin.

2. Sprinkle both sides of the pork with salt and pepper.

3. Set up three shallow bowls: In the first, season ½ cup of the flour with salt and pepper. In the second, whisk the milk and egg together. In the third, place the panko. Dredge the pork scallops in the seasoned flour, shaking off the excess . . .

4. Then quickly dunk the pork into the milk-egg mixture . . .

The secret's in the sauce!

5. Then finally coat it in the panko.

6. In a large skillet, heat the oil and 4 tablespoons of the butter over medium heat. Add the pork scallops . . .

7. And cook until golden and crisp, 2 to 2½ minutes per side.

8. Remove them to a plate lined with paper towels.

9. Add the remaining 2 tablespoons butter and the capers to the skillet and whisk to scrape any browned bits from the bottom of the pan.

10. Sprinkle the remaining 2 tablespoons flour into the skillet . . .

11. And whisk and cook until the roux starts to turn deep golden, about 2 minutes.

12. Pour in the wine . . .

13. And the chicken broth . . .

14. And whisk and cook until the sauce is smooth and thin, 3 to 4 minutes.

15. Squeeze in the lemon juice . . .

16. Then stir and taste the sauce, adjusting the seasonings as needed.

17. To serve, arrange a bed of arugula on a platter. Set the pork and lemon wedges over the arugula and top with Parmesan shavings and a sprinkle of parsley. Pour on the sauce just before serving with Loaded Crash Hots on the side.

. . . .

VARIATIONS

» *Use chicken cutlets instead of pork chops for a more classic dish.*

» *Serve the pork and sauce over rice or pasta.*

» *Add ¼ cup heavy cream at the end of the sauce-cooking process for a creamier sauce.*

LOADED CRASH HOTS

MAKES 2 OR 3 SERVINGS

Crash Hot Potatoes were one of the earliest recipes I shared on my website many years ago, and it remains one of the top five potato recipes in my repertoire. I usually serve them plain and holy, with nothing but a sprinkle of kosher salt and pepper. But they're even more amazing with cheese, bacon, sour cream, and chives! You'll never go back to plain baked potatoes again. (Or if you do, you won't be as into them. Sorry, baked potatoes!)

6 small round yellow or red potatoes

Kosher salt

3 tablespoons olive oil, plus more for the masher

Black pepper

⅓ cup grated cheddar cheese

¼ cup sour cream

2 slices thick-cut bacon, cooked and chopped

1 teaspoon chopped fresh chives

1. Preheat the oven to 475°F.

2. In a medium saucepan of boiling salted water, cook the potatoes until fork-tender, about 12 minutes.

3. Transfer the potatoes to a small sheet pan and brush a potato masher with some of the olive oil.

4. Press to flatten the potatoes halfway, then rotate the masher and flatten them more. Brush the masher with more oil as you go to prevent sticking.

5. Generously brush the tops with more olive oil and sprinkle with salt and pepper.

6. Transfer to the oven and bake until browned and crisp around the edges, about 15 minutes.

7. Top each potato with cheddar, sour cream, and bacon . . .

8. And finish with a sprinkling of chives.

Boiled, smashed, baked, and loaded!

Pepperoni Fried Rice

MAKES 6 SERVINGS

Some food mash-ups are weird. Some are delicious. And, as is the case with this lightning-fast stir-fry, some are weirdly delicious! This throw-together skillet dish, which is part fried rice and part pepperoni-and-pineapple pizza, should not be as delicious as it is. But it is! It absolutely, positively is!

This is one mash-up that'll rock your world.

Stir-fry meets pizza!

2 tablespoons olive oil

1 medium onion, thinly sliced

1 green bell pepper, cut into large squares

2 garlic cloves, minced

One 5-ounce package mini pepperoni (or regular pepperoni, chopped)

¼ cup jarred pizza or marinara sauce

1 teaspoon red pepper flakes

3 cups microwave white rice, heated according to the package directions

One 8-ounce can pineapple chunks, drained

1 cup mozzarella pearls or cubed fresh mozzarella cheese

¼ cup fresh basil leaves

1. In a large cast-iron skillet, heat the olive oil over medium-high heat. Add the onion, bell pepper, garlic, and pepperoni . . .

4. And stir until everything is coated in the sauce, another minute.

7. Add the pineapple chunks and stir them in to heat up, about 1 minute.

2. And stir and cook until the onion has softened and the pepperoni is starting to sizzle, about 3 minutes.

5. Add the rice . . .

8. Add the mozzarella at the very last minute and stir!

3. Add the pizza sauce and pepper flakes . . .

6. And cook, stirring constantly, until the rice is sizzling and hot, 2 to 3 minutes.

9. You'll want to serve it immediately so that the mozzarella is very soft but still intact. Garnish with fresh basil leaves and fall in love!

Salmon Burgers

MAKES 4 SERVINGS

"Salmon burger" is a phrase that's generally in the same category as "meatloaf" in the sense that you kinda need to look past the words and just focus on how delicious the dish is. To make these salmon burgers, I use good ol' canned salmon (come to think of it, "canned salmon" is another one of those phrases), which makes this a super-handy, super-easy way to whip up a seafood supper at a moment's notice! And you can use whatever canned salmon you're used to; there are cheap options and more pricey options, and there's no wrong answer. These burgers are truly tasty!

SALMON PATTIES

1 large egg

2 tablespoons mayonnaise

1 tablespoon whole-grain mustard

1 teaspoon seafood seasoning (preferably Old Bay)

Juice of ½ lemon

A few dashes of hot sauce

Two 6-ounce cans pink salmon in water, drained

½ cup panko breadcrumbs

4 green onions, thinly sliced

Pinch of kosher salt

½ teaspoon black pepper

2 tablespoons olive oil

2 tablespoons salted butter

CAPER MAYO

½ cup mayonnaise

2 teaspoons chopped capers

Juice of ½ lemon

Hot sauce

Kosher salt and black pepper

TO ASSEMBLE

4 whole wheat hamburger buns, toasted

Green leaf or red leaf lettuce

Sliced tomato

Pickle slices

Chips and/or raw vegetables, for serving

3. Add the (very very fancy) canned salmon . . .

4. Along with the panko . . .

1. Make the salmon patties: In a medium bowl, combine the egg, mayonnaise, mustard, seafood seasoning, lemon juice, and hot sauce . . .

2. And mix until smooth.

5. The green onions, salt, and pepper . . .

Made with canned salmon!
Who knew?

6. And fold the mixture until combined.

7. Divide the mixture into 4 equal portions and shape into patties (it's very easy to handle!). Set them on a plate.

8. In a large skillet, heat the olive oil and butter over medium-high heat. Add the salmon patties and cook until browned on one side . . .

9. Then flip and cook until completely hot in the middle and golden and crisp on the second side, about 4 minutes total. Remove from the heat.

10. Make the caper mayo: In a small bowl, combine the mayo, capers, lemon juice, and hot sauce, salt, and pepper to taste . . .

11. And stir to mix!

12. To assemble: Spread each half of the hamburger buns generously with the caper mayo.

13. Add a leaf of lettuce to the bottom bun, then a salmon patty . . .

14. And top with tomato and pickles! It's a winning combo.

15. Serve with chips and veggies on the side.

. . . .

VARIATIONS

» *Serve the patties without the buns, alongside a salad. A lovely light lunch!*

» *Serve mini patties as an appetizer with the caper mayo as a dipping sauce.*

Steak Pizzaiola

MAKES 6 GENEROUS SERVINGS

My oh my, this is my kind of eating. And it's definitely my kind of cooking! It's pronounced (roughly) "Steak Pizz-aye-OH-la" and means "steak in pizza sauce." I'm always amazed at how fancy and complicated the finished dish looks, yet how gosh darn quick and easy it is to pull together. And it's one of those amazing dishes that's just as perfect for dinner guests as it is for teenage boys.

I just described 90 percent of my favorite recipes right there. Teenage boys are the best!

3 ciabatta rolls, halved horizontally

6 tablespoons olive oil

3 Kansas City strip steaks (¾ inch to 1 inch thick), about 12 ounces each

Kosher salt and black pepper

1 large yellow onion, sliced thick

One 16-ounce jar sliced roasted red peppers, drained

6 garlic cloves, thinly sliced

½ teaspoon red pepper flakes

2 tablespoons tomato paste

½ cup red wine (or beef broth)

One 14.5-ounce can stewed tomatoes

One 15-ounce can tomato sauce

¼ cup drained sliced pepperoncini

1 tablespoon fresh oregano leaves (or 1 teaspoon dried)

2 tablespoons grated Parmesan cheese, plus more to taste

2 tablespoons chopped fresh flat-leaf parsley

1. Preheat the oven to 425°F.

2. Place the rolls cut side up on a sheet pan and brush with 4 tablespoons (¼ cup) of the olive oil.

3. Toast them in the oven until golden brown, about 12 minutes. Set aside.

4. In a large cast-iron skillet, heat the remaining 2 tablespoons olive oil over medium-high heat. Season the steaks with salt and pepper, then add them to the skillet.

5. Cook to your desired doneness, about 4 minutes per side for medium-rare. Remove them to a cutting board and cover them with foil to keep warm.

6. To the same skillet, add the onion, roasted red peppers, garlic, and pepper flakes . . .

7. And cook, stirring constantly, until the onions have started to soften, about 3 minutes.

8. Add the tomato paste and cook, stirring, for about 30 seconds.

9. Pour in the wine (which is always a miraculous moment!) . . .

10. And scrape the bottom of the pan to deglaze.

11. Add the stewed tomatoes, tomato sauce, and pepperoncini . . .

12. And the oregano . . .

13. And stir and let simmer for about 10 minutes to allow everything to get married and have babies, then remove from the heat.

14. Slice the steak and place it over the sauce . . .

15. Then sprinkle the top with the Parmesan and parsley.

16. Serve the steak and sauce over a ciabatta roll half. Top with more Parmesan if you'd like!

. . . .

VARIATIONS

» *Serve the steak and sauce over rigatoni instead of rolls.*

» *Substitute boneless, skinless chicken breasts for the steak.*

» *Stir 1 cup ricotta cheese into the sauce right before adding the steak.*

Steak + Pizza Sauce = Yes!

Chicken with Mustard Herb Sauce

MAKES 4 SERVINGS

I love this category of recipes! The basic steps are as follows: Cook some kind of protein (chicken, pork, beef, fish) in butter and oil, then remove it from the pan. Make a sauce in the same pan. Return the protein to the sauce. There are a million delicious ways to pull this off, but this one, with flavorful chicken cutlets and a tangy mustard sauce, is hard to beat. It's delicious on its own or with mashed potatoes, but when served on a bed of garlicky spinach, it's basically too good for color TV, to paraphrase the line in *Steel Magnolias*. There's never been a bigger winner of a chicken dinner!

Four 6-ounce boneless, skinless chicken breasts, halved horizontally (to create 8 chicken cutlets)

Kosher salt and black pepper

4 tablespoons (½ stick) salted butter

1 tablespoon olive oil

3 garlic cloves, minced

¾ cup dry white wine (or low-sodium chicken broth)

1½ cups low-sodium chicken broth, plus more as needed

3 heaping tablespoons grainy mustard

½ cup chopped mixed fresh herbs, such as dill, parsley, and chives, plus more for garnish

Lemon-Garlic Spinach (page 231), for serving

1. Season both sides of the chicken with salt and pepper.

2. In a large (mine is very large!) skillet, heat 2 tablespoons of the butter and the olive oil over medium-high heat. Add the chicken cutlets (working in batches if necessary) and cook until golden brown and cooked through, about 3 minutes per side.

3. Remove the cutlets to a plate and set aside.

4. Add the garlic to the skillet and stir it for about 30 seconds to release the flavor.

5. Pour in the wine, stirring as you pour to scrape up the browned bits from the bottom of the skillet. Let it simmer to reduce by about half, about 2 minutes.

6. Reduce the heat to medium and add the broth . . .

Easy meets elegant!

7. And the mustard!

8. Stir for 2 to 3 minutes to let the mixture thicken.

9. Add the remaining 2 tablespoons butter, stirring to melt. Season with salt and pepper to taste.

10. Reduce the heat to low, add the chopped herbs, and stir them in.

11. Return the chicken to the skillet (making sure to pour any juices on the plate back into the pan) . . .

12. And spoon the sauce over the chicken so there's plenty of mustardy, herby goodness all over.

13. Serve the chicken on a bed of Lemon-Garlic Spinach, with extra fresh herbs on top.

VARIATIONS

» *Use boneless pork chops instead of chicken.*

» *Instead of adding butter to the sauce toward the end, splash in 3 tablespoons heavy cream for a mustard cream sauce.*

» *Use a mustard with more spice to give the sauce a nice kick.*

We're a very professional TV crew.

LEMON-GARLIC SPINACH

MAKES 4 TO 6 SERVINGS

2 tablespoons olive oil

2 garlic cloves, minced

Two 10-ounce packages baby spinach

Kosher salt and black pepper

Juice of ½ lemon

1. In a large, high-sided skillet, heat the olive oil over medium-high heat. Add the garlic and give it a quick stir.

2. Add the spinach (the pan will be very full!) . . .

3. And use tongs to toss it around as it starts to cook and wilt.

4. When the spinach is about halfway wilted, add salt and pepper to taste and the lemon juice. Give it one last toss and turn off the heat. (You want the spinach to still have a little body.) Serve warm.

Chicken with bruschetta topping!

Bruschetta Chicken

MAKES 3 TO 6 SERVINGS

It's hard to see that there's actually chicken in that thar pan, and that is because of all the delicious topping that's covering it up! This is sautéed chicken covered with a deconstructed bruschetta-type mix of crisp bread, tomatoes, garlic, basil . . . the whole shebang. It's good. It's glorious! And you will gobble up that topping like no one's business.

½ loaf crusty French bread, cut into ¼-inch cubes

5 tablespoons olive oil

Kosher salt and black pepper

2 tablespoons salted butter

6 chicken cutlets (thin-cut chicken breasts)

5 Roma tomatoes, diced

2 garlic cloves, pressed

12 fresh basil leaves, cut into a chiffonade, plus small whole leaves for garnish

2 tablespoons balsamic glaze, plus more for serving

4 ounces goat cheese

1. Preheat the oven to 375°F.

2. Spread the bread on the sheet pan and drizzle on 3 tablespoons of the olive oil. Sprinkle with salt and pepper . . .

4. And set the croutons aside to cool.

6. And cook until nice and golden on one side, about 3 minutes. Flip to the other side and cook for about another 2 minutes, until cooked through. Turn off the heat.

5. In a large heavy skillet, heat the remaining 2 tablespoons olive oil and the butter over medium-high heat. Season the chicken with salt and pepper. Place the chicken in the pan . . .

3. And toss everything to coat. Bake until crisp, about 7 minutes . . .

7. In a medium bowl, combine the tomatoes, garlic, basil chiffonade, and balsamic glaze.

8. Add the croutons . . .

9. And stir everything together.

10. Spoon the topping all over the chicken . . .

11. Then crumble on the goat cheese. Garnish with small basil leaves and drizzle with a little balsamic glaze. Delicious!

Heaven is walking with my dogs!

Chicken Curry in a Hurry

MAKES 6 TO 8 SERVINGS

This is the quickest way to satisfy your curry cravings . . . and you should listen to me, because I have curry cravings about four times a week. (Okay, four times a day!) It doesn't matter how many times I've whipped up this crazy-fast curry stew; I still sit down with a bowl and slowly savor every bite, even if I'm in a hurry . . . which, given the name of this recipe, is a little ironic!

2 tablespoons salted butter

4 garlic cloves, minced

1 medium yellow onion, finely diced

1 cup frozen sweet potato (or 1 sweet potato, peeled and finely diced)

¼ teaspoon kosher salt, plus more to taste

Pinch of black pepper

2 tablespoons curry powder

1 teaspoon ground turmeric

1½ cups chicken broth

One 13.5-ounce can full-fat coconut milk

2 tablespoons honey

3 cups shredded cooked chicken (see page xxi)

2 tablespoons sriracha

Juice of 1 lime, plus lime wedges for serving

¼ cup fresh cilantro leaves, chopped, plus more for garnish

½ small mango, diced (or jarred diced mango), for garnish

1. In a large skillet, combine the butter, garlic, onion, sweet potato, salt, and pepper . . .

3. Sprinkle the curry powder and turmeric on top . . .

5. Add the chicken broth and coconut milk . . .

2. And cook and stir over medium-high heat until the onion starts to turn translucent, about 3 minutes.

4. Then stir and cook for another minute to awaken all the amazing flavor!

6. And stir to combine.

7. Add the honey and let it come to a gentle simmer, about 3 more minutes.

8. Stir in the shredded chicken . . .

9. Then add the sriracha and lime juice and stir.

10. The essential ingredient: cilantro! Stir it in and remove the skillet from the heat.

11. Ladle a generous portion into a bowl and sprinkle the mango on the top . . .

12. Along with plenty of cilantro. Serve with lime wedges!

- -

VARIATIONS

» *Serve over basmati or jasmine rice.*

» *Add diced red bell pepper to the skillet with the onion and sweet potato if you'd like a little more color.*

» *Substitute veggie broth for the chicken broth and chickpeas for the chicken for a vegetarian version.*

Live, love, laugh!

Super-fast stew!

LOVIN' FROM THE OVEN

Casseroles, hot dishes, bakes . . . whatever you call them, they are the stars of church potlucks everywhere. They're also the stars of my kitchen; there's just something so satisfying about throwing a mix of ingredients into a baking pan and slapping it into the oven for a period of time. It's strangely the same sense of satisfaction I get when I throw all my dirty dishes in a sink of soapy water and walk away (sometimes for many hours, but that's another story for another time). These amazingly comforting recipes, from casseroles to sheet pan suppers and a couple of gems in between, make the oven do most of the work.

Cheesy Green Bean and Rice Casserole

MAKES 12 TO 16 SERVINGS

Heads up! This casserole is absolutely ridiculous. For one, the sauce is rich, creamy, and delicious, with mushrooms, garlic, and cheddar cheese. For another, it's made with ready-to-go convenience ingredients such as frozen diced onions, bagged microwave rice, and frozen green beans! But somehow the two worlds meet in a scrumptious casserole that's as at home on a Thanksgiving table as it is at Tuesday night supper. You'll love how easy this baby is to assemble and get in the oven. It's delicious!

This can be served alongside any main protein, or as a main dish with a salad! (Or as a late-night snack after a football game. Don't ask me how I know this.)

SAUCE

4 slices bacon, finely chopped

½ cup frozen diced onion

2 garlic cloves, peeled

6 ounces white mushrooms, chopped

1 teaspoon Italian seasoning

½ teaspoon cayenne pepper

Kosher salt and black pepper

Two 10.5-ounce cans condensed cream of mushroom soup

1 cup vegetable broth

8 ounces Velveeta, cut into cubes

1½ cups grated cheddar cheese

CASSEROLE

Two 8.8-ounce packets microwaveable white rice

3 cups frozen green beans

1 large jar diced pimientos

1 cup grated cheddar cheese

2 cups fried onions (such as French's)

Minced fresh flat-leaf parsley, for garnish

1. Preheat the oven to 375°F.

2. Make the sauce: In a medium skillet, cook the bacon over medium-high heat until most of the fat is rendered and the bacon is golden, 3 to 4 minutes. Pour off most of the bacon fat.

3. Add the frozen onions . . .

4. Then grate in the garlic . . .

5. And add the mushrooms, Italian seasoning, cayenne, and salt and black pepper to taste.

Super-easy ingredients!

6. Stir and cook until the mushrooms are starting to get tender, 4 to 5 minutes.

7. Reduce the heat to medium, add the canned soup and broth . . .

8. And stir and cook until very hot, 2 to 3 more minutes.

9. Add the Velveeta and cheddar . . .

10. And stir until the cheeses are melted. Taste and adjust the seasonings.

11. Assemble the casserole: Pour the rice into a 9 x 13-inch baking dish. (No need to microwave the rice first!)

12. Add the green beans (right out of the bag!) and the pimientos . . .

13. And stir to mix everything together.

14. Pour the sauce on top! My goodness.

15. Lightly give everything a stir (no need to totally mix together).

16. Sprinkle on the cheddar and the fried onions.

16. Bake until golden on top and bubbling around the edges, about 30 minutes. (Watch the top so that it doesn't get too brown.) Sprinkle the parsley on top before serving.

A HAPPY MOMENT

Ladd had a serious accident on the ranch while fighting wildfire a couple of months before Alex's wedding, and he was still wearing a big ol' neck brace on the big day. Fortunately, the doctor had told him he could take off the brace to walk her down the aisle (and have the first dance!), so he was happy to have a few brace-free photos. As for me, I was just darn grateful that Ladd could even be at Alex's wedding, and while I was able to resist getting emotional for most of the significant moments of the wedding, it was their dance that did me in. Many Kleenex were required!

Spinach Ravioli Bake

MAKES 8 TO 12 SERVINGS

This is my new favorite kind of casserole. It requires almost zero prep or time, and the whole thing is assembled right in the baking dish. I don't know how it all comes together into such a delectable finished dish, but it just does. Store-bought ravioli, boxed spinach, jarred sauce, grated cheese, prepared pesto . . . a combination that results in celebration!

Two 10-ounce packages fresh or frozen cheese ravioli, cooked for half the recommended time and drained

4 cups baby spinach

One 24-ounce jar vodka sauce

2 cups grated mozzarella cheese

One 5-ounce jar pesto

1. Preheat the oven to 400°F.

2. Pour the ravioli into a 9 x 13-inch baking dish.

4. Then pour the vodka sauce all over the spinach.

6. And dot the pesto all over the cheese.

3. Spread the spinach all over the top of the ravioli . . .

5. Sprinkle the mozzarella all over the sauce . . .

7. Bake until the cheese is bubbling, 25 to 30 minutes. Serve by the (generous) spoonful!

Assembled right in the baking dish!

Teriyaki Chicken Sheet Pan Supper

MAKES 8 SERVINGS

Sticky chicken thighs and colorful veggies headline this incredibly easy sheet pan supper that I never, ever get tired of. Using bottled teriyaki sauce eliminates mixing a sauce from scratch, and the charred, caramelized edges send the flavor of this meal into the stratosphere!

1 bunch asparagus, ends trimmed, cut into 2-inch pieces

8 green onions, halved lengthwise, and cut crosswise into 1-inch pieces

1 head broccoli, cut into small florets

12 tricolor mini peppers, stemmed and halved lengthwise

1 large red onion, cut into large chunks

1½ cups (12 ounces) teriyaki sauce

8 boneless, skinless chicken thighs

Grated zest of 1 lime

Sesame seeds, for garnish

Cilantro leaves, for garnish

1. Preheat the oven to 400°F. Line a sheet pan with foil.

2. Place all the veggies on the sheet pan and drizzle on ¾ cup of the teriyaki sauce. Split the remaining ¾ cup sauce between two bowls.

4. Arrange the chicken thighs on top of the veggies . . .

6. Bake the chicken and veggies for 15 minutes. (Wash the brush while the chicken bakes.)

3. Toss the veggies to coat them in the sauce.

5. And brush the sauce from one of the bowls all over the chicken.

7. After the 15 minutes, with a clean brush, brush the chicken with the sauce from the second bowl. Turn on the oven broiler.

8. Broil until part of the sauce starts to caramelize on the chicken, 3 to 4 minutes. Watch it carefully to make sure it doesn't burn!

9. Zest the lime all over the chicken and veggies . . .

10. And sprinkle with sesame seeds and cilantro. Divide onto plates and dive in!

VARIATIONS

» *Mix the teriyaki with minced garlic and hot chile oil to bump up the flavor and heat.*

» *Use chicken drumsticks instead of thighs.*

» *Serve over rice or noodles for a heartier meal!*

Ready in 30!

Cheesy Kale Casserole

MAKES 6 SERVINGS

This recipe will make you laugh. In what universe does a person like me believe that it's an accepted practice to bake two kinds of wholesome, healthy kale in a skillet full of creamy sauce and top it with approximately nine hundred pounds of cheese?

This universe, evidently. And while I'd love to apologize for it, I'm too busy looking at these photos and remembering how amazing it is! This makes a glorious side dish for steak or chicken . . . or a main course with a loaf of crusty bread and a tomato salad!

1½ cups heavy cream

One 8-ounce container mascarpone

½ small onion, thinly sliced

2 garlic cloves, thinly sliced

Grated zest of 1 lemon

1 teaspoon smoked paprika

Pinch of ground nutmeg

Kosher salt and black pepper

2 bunches Tuscan (lacinato) kale, stemmed and torn into pieces

2 small or 1 large bunch curly kale, stemmed and torn into pieces

½ cup panko breadcrumbs

4 tablespoons (½ stick) salted butter, melted

3 cups grated Fontina or Monterey Jack cheese

1. Preheat the oven to 425°F.

2. In a large Dutch oven, combine the cream and mascarpone . . .

4. The lemon zest and smoked paprika . . .

6. Bring the mixture to a simmer over medium heat and cook until the onion is soft and the mixture is very fragrant, 10 to 12 minutes.

3. The onion and garlic . . .

5. And the nutmeg and salt and pepper to taste.

7. Add all the kale. It should be overflowing! Press it down as much as you can . . .

I'll take my cheese with a little kale, please!

8. Then put the lid on the pan and let the greens cook for 3 minutes.

9. While the greens are cooking, in a small bowl, mix the panko and melted butter. Add a pinch of salt and pepper.

10. Give the greens a stir. They should be just about halfway wilted!

11. Pour the mixture into a 10-inch cast-iron skillet, making sure to get all the creamy sauce in the pan.

12. Top the greens with the grated cheese . . .

13. And sprinkle the buttery crumbs over the top.

14. Place on a sheet pan and bake until the crumbs are golden and the cheese is bubbling, 18 to 20 minutes. Let it sit 10 minutes before serving.

CHANGE IT UP!

Substitute any combination of dark, leafy greens for the kale—or mix it in with the kale! Collard greens, Swiss chard, and spinach are perfect add-ins. If you'd like some color in the dish, add a cup of diced roasted red peppers from a jar! And of course, change up the cheese however you wish. Love this dish!

Meatball and Polenta Casserole

MAKES 8 TO 10 SERVINGS

My gosh, is this an amazing casserole! Now, trust me—there are a few steps, but there are also a few short-cuts that turn what could be an incredibly complicated dish into a really darn delicious dinner in less than an hour. Preformed meatballs (my favorite new item from the meat department), premade polenta, and a couple of pan-saving (and time-saving) steps will make this a favorite of yours! It sure is a favorite of mine.

One 28-ounce can diced tomatoes

3 garlic cloves, minced

¼ cup olive oil

8 fresh basil leaves, torn

2 tablespoons fresh oregano leaves

Kosher salt and black pepper

20 uncooked store-bought meatballs (or your own from-scratch meatballs!)

4 tablespoons (½ stick) salted butter

1 onion, thinly sliced

One 18-ounce tube polenta

1 cup ricotta cheese

¾ cup grated Parmesan cheese

1 cup heavy cream

Tossed salad and garlic bread, for serving

1. Preheat the oven to 425°F.

2. In a 9 x 13-inch baking dish, combine the canned tomatoes, garlic, and olive oil.

3. Drop in the torn basil and 1 tablespoon of the oregano leaves.

4. Stir to mix the sauce . . .

5. Then season with salt and pepper to taste and stir.

6. Arrange the meatballs in the sauce and bake for 15 minutes.

7. While the meatballs are in the oven, in a large pot, melt the butter over medium-high heat. Add the onion and the remaining 1 tablespoon oregano.

8. Stir and cook the onions until they start to turn translucent, about 3 minutes.

9. Crumble in the polenta. (If it's too firm to crumble, you can grate it using the large grater holes!)

10. Add the ricotta . . .

11. ½ cup of the Parmesan . . .

12. And the cream.

13. Stir vigorously while it heats, breaking up the polenta until it's the consistency of mashed potatoes. Season with salt and pepper to taste.

14. When the meatballs are finished baking . . .

15. Transfer them to a separate bowl, along with most of the sauce.

16. Pour the polenta into the pan—don't clean the pan! You want it a little saucy—and spread it into an even layer.

17. Arrange the meatballs and sauce over the polenta . . .

18. And sprinkle on the remaining ¼ cup Parmesan!

19. Bake until bubbling around the edges and very hot, about 30 minutes. Serve with a side salad and garlic bread!

• •

VARIATIONS

» *Skip the polenta and serve the meatballs in deli rolls.*

» *Serve the meatballs over mashed potatoes or with The Best Fettuccine Alfredo (page 176) instead!*

Pre-formed meatballs are baked in the sauce!

Veggie Tot Pie

MAKES 6 TO 8 SERVINGS

A tot pie is just like a pot pie but instead of pie crust or biscuits, it's topped with beautiful frozen tots! A typical pot pie has a chicken and veggie mixture, but this one's meatless just for fun. Also, to keep things really exciting, I set out to make the sauce almost entirely from freezer and pantry staples . . . and I regret to inform you that the results were absolutely delicious.

Note: One beauty of this recipe is that you can mix or sub in whatever frozen vegetables you like! My favorite combo is below, but suit your family—and yourself!

1 tablespoon salted butter

½ cup frozen diced onion

1 cup frozen green beans

1 cup frozen butternut squash chunks

½ cup frozen roasted corn

½ cup frozen peas

One 4-ounce jar pimientos, drained

1 tablespoon garlic paste or 2 garlic cloves, grated

One 10.5-ounce can condensed cream of mushroom soup

One 10.5-ounce can condensed cream of celery soup

Kosher salt and black pepper

Pinch of ground turmeric

One 32-ounce bag frozen Tater Tots, thawed

2 tablespoons chopped fresh parsley

1. Preheat the oven to 450°F.

2. In a large ovenproof skillet, melt the butter over medium-high heat. Add the onion . . .

4. The roasted corn, peas . . .

6. Add the garlic. (I used garlic paste! It's so wonderfully weird!)

3. The green beans, butternut squash . . .

5. And the pimientos.

7. Cook the veggies for 10 minutes, stirring often, to heat them through.

Almost everything's from the freezer!

8. Add the mushroom soup . . .

9. The celery soup and 1 soup can of water.

10. Stir as the mixture heats and begins to bubble, about 5 minutes . . .

11. Then add salt and pepper to taste and the turmeric.

12. When it's hot and steaming, turn off the heat.

13. Arrange the frozen tots in a circular pattern, completely covering the sauce. (No need to press them down!)

14. Bake the tot pie until the tots are golden and crisp and the edges are bubbling, about 30 minutes.

15. Sprinkle on the parsley to garnish.

Happiness is a Lab named Lucy!

Sheet Pan Meatloaf

MAKES 8 TO 12 SERVINGS

I have well established my undying love for meatloaf. I think it's the most underrated dinner in the history of mankind, and when meatloaf is good, it's just *soooooo* good. The only downside of meatloaf (well, besides its name) is that, because of its loafy shape, it can take an inordinately long time to bake in the oven. Enter: sheet pan meatloaf, which brings you all the flavorful, meaty, saucy goodness in a fraction of the baking time. I speak from experience here: It's very hard to go back to the original after seeing what a cinch this is!

I love to serve this with a simple roasted broccoli and another oven favorite, Sheet Pan Mac and Cheese (page 184). Total comfort food!

MEATLOAF

6 slices white sandwich bread

1 cup whole milk

Cooking spray

½ cup plain breadcrumbs

3 pounds ground beef

1 cup grated Parmesan cheese

4 large eggs, whisked

½ cup minced fresh flat-leaf parsley, plus more for garnish

1½ teaspoons seasoned salt (such as Lawry's)

Black pepper

Garlic-Parmesan Roasted Broccoli (page 261), for serving

GLAZE

1 cup ketchup

½ cup packed brown sugar

2 tablespoons balsamic vinegar

1 tablespoon Worcestershire sauce

6 slices bacon (not thick-cut), cooked to crisp and roughly chopped

1. Preheat the oven to 400°F.

2. Make the meatloaf: Place the bread in a large bowl and pour the milk on top. Let it sit for 5 minutes to soak it all up.

4. Shake the pan to get the breadcrumbs to spread out and stick to the spray.

6. Then sprinkle in the seasoned salt and black pepper to taste.

3. Generously mist a sheet pan with cooking spray, then sprinkle the breadcrumbs on top.

5. To the bowl with the soaked bread, add the ground beef, Parmesan, eggs, and parsley.

7. Use your hands or a wooden spoon to mix everything together, then set aside.

8. Now make the glaze: In a small bowl, combine the ketchup, brown sugar, balsamic, and Worcestershire . . .

10. Drop large spoons of the meat mixture all over the breadcrumb-coated sheet pan . . .

12. Brush half of the glaze all over the surface, getting into the cracks and crevices.

9. And whisk until smooth.

11. And pat/press it into an even layer, reaching out to the edges of the pan (it will shrink when it bakes!).

13. Sprinkle the bacon all over the top.

14. Bake the meatloaf for 20 minutes, then brush on the remaining glaze and broil for 2 to 3 minutes, taking care not to burn it. Perfection!

When did Bryce grow up?!?

15. Cut it into squares and sprinkle on some minced parsley. Serve with Garlic-Parmesan Roasted Broccoli.

More saucy surface area!
(And it cooks faster!)

GARLIC-PARMESAN ROASTED BROCCOLI

MAKES 4 TO 6 SERVINGS

I love broccoli best when it's roasted and the little trees have some blackened areas. It reminds me of the time one of our neighbors did some aerial weed spraying on a windy day many years ago. Don't worry—my trees are just fine now, our neighbors are still friends, and I'm sorry I got away from the main point, which is that this is an easy and tasty way to get your broccoli, baby!

¼ cup olive oil

5 garlic cloves

1 pound broccoli, broken up into florets

Kosher salt and black pepper

½ lemon

⅔ cup shredded Parmesan cheese

1. Preheat the oven to 425°F.

2. Pour the olive oil into a small bowl and press the garlic through a garlic press into the oil.

3. Mix it together with a fork.

4. Place the broccoli on a small sheet pan (this one is a quarter sheet) and pour the garlic oil on top.

5. Sprinkle on salt and pepper to taste . . .

6. And toss it all together.

7. Bake until the broccoli is starting to brown around the edges, about 10 minutes.

8. Squeeze the lemon juice all over . . .

9. Then sprinkle the Parmesan on top!

10. Return to the oven for 5 to 7 minutes to melt the Parmesan. If you like the Parmesan to be more browned and crisp, lean more toward the 7-minute mark. Toss, then serve!

Baked, not fried!

General Tso's Chicken

MAKES 2 TO 4 SERVINGS

General Tso's Chicken is a classic dish on menus in Chinese restaurants across the United States, and I always love how sticky, spicy, and rich in color it is. I've made General Tso's recipes in the past that call for frying the chicken in oil before coating it in the sauce, but I love baking the chicken in the oven while the sauce cooks on the stove. It's a time-saver and a mess-saver, and it's so incredibly tasty.

Win, win, and win!

1 cup all-purpose flour

3 large eggs

4 tablespoons soy sauce

2 cups panko breadcrumbs

1½ pounds boneless, skinless chicken breast, cut into 1- to 2-inch cubes

Cooking spray

2 teaspoons toasted sesame oil

2 garlic cloves, finely minced

1 teaspoon grated fresh ginger

Pinch of red pepper flakes

3 tablespoons hoisin sauce

2 tablespoons rice vinegar

¾ cup low-sodium chicken broth

2 teaspoons cornstarch

2 tablespoons sriracha

Cooked white rice, brown rice, or noodles, for serving

Sliced green onions, for serving

1. Preheat the oven to 425°F.

2. Set up a three-bowl assembly line: Put the flour in the first bowl, mix the egg with 2 tablespoons of the soy sauce in the second bowl, and put the panko in the third bowl.

3. Bread the chicken by dropping the pieces one at a time into the flour . . .

4. The egg-soy mixture . . .

5. And the panko.

6. Set the breaded chicken on a rack placed over a baking sheet and mist them with cooking spray. Bake until the chicken is crisp and barely starting to turn golden brown, 15 to 17 minutes.

7. While the chicken is baking, in a large skillet, combine the sesame oil, garlic, ginger, and pepper flakes.

8. Stir and cook over medium heat until fragrant (that means it smells dang good), about 1 minute.

10. And whisk until the mixture is bubbling.

12. Then pour it into the pan . . .

9. Add the hoisin, vinegar, and remaining 2 tablespoons soy sauce . . .

11. In a spouted cup, whisk the chicken broth with the cornstarch until it's totally combined . . .

13. Along with the sriracha . . .

Fred, the wedding crasher!

14. And whisk until the sauce is combined. Let it simmer . . .

15. Until it's thick and glossy. (If it appears overly thick, splash in ¼ cup water and stir.) Turn off the heat.

16. Add the baked chicken to the sauce and gently toss . . .

17. Until the chicken is totally coated in sauce.

18. Serve hot over rice or noodles and garnish with green onions . . . or just put it on a plate. It speaks for itself!

We love dogs around here!

Low-Effort Lasagna

MAKES 9 TO 12 SERVINGS

I originally created this recipe when I had promised my boys lasagna and I had less than an hour to pull it off because I had procrastinated by watching TikTok videos . . . I mean by being absorbed in yet another Dostoevsky novel. I laughed as I made it the first time, because I cooked absolutely nothing and assembled everything right in the pan with zero effort whatsoever. Fast-forward . . . I've made this probably ten times since. It's totally cheating, and while it probably isn't as over-the-top fabulous as a from-scratch lasagna, it's pretty darn amazing considering how fast it comes together. Try it! You'll laugh and you'll adore it.

4 cups jarred marinara sauce

One 9-ounce box no-boil lasagna noodles

12 ounces ricotta cheese

Kosher salt and black pepper

One 8-ounce jar pesto

18 slices mozzarella cheese

2 cups packaged precooked crumbled sausage (such as Jimmy Dean)

12 frozen meatballs, thawed and finely diced

3 pinches of garlic powder

3 pinches of red pepper flakes

1 cup grated Parmesan cheese

2 tablespoons chopped fresh parsley

1. Preheat the oven to 350°F.

2. Cover the bottom of a lasagna pan with about 1 cup of the marinara.

4. Then cover the noodles with one-third of the ricotta.

6. Then spoon on one-third of the pesto.

3. Overlap 4 of the no-boil noodles . . .

5. Sprinkle the ricotta with salt and pepper to taste . . .

7. Arrange 6 slices of the mozzarella in a layer on top of the pesto.

Assembled right in the pan—no pre-cooking of ingredients!

8. Mix together the sausage crumbles and diced meatballs and spoon one-third of the mixture over the mozzarella.

11. Sprinkle the Parmesan over the marinara and transfer to the oven.

9. Then more salt and black pepper! Sprinkle on a pinch each of garlic powder and red pepper flakes.

12. Bake until hot and bubbling, about 30 minutes.

13. Sprinkle with parsley. Let it sit 10 minutes, then cut into squares and serve!

10. Repeat these layers twice (1 cup marinara, noodles, ricotta, salt and pepper, pesto, mozzarella, meat, garlic powder, red pepper flakes), ending with the final 1 cup marinara.

Hey, didn't we just walk down the aisle . . . twenty-five years ago?

Meaty Lazy Chiles Rellenos

MAKES 6 TO 8 SERVINGS

This is a meaty version of my mom's old lazy chiles rellenos casserole, with flavorful, spicy ground beef as a welcome addition! This is the kind of food the ladies in my church would make for the youth group when I was growing up, as it wasn't fancy and it fed a crowd. The whole green chiles really make this casserole something special; get some good Hatch ones if you're able!

1 pound lean ground beef

1 teaspoon onion powder

1 tablespoon plus ½ teaspoon chili powder

1½ teaspoons kosher salt

2 garlic cloves, pressed in a garlic press

½ cup jarred salsa, plus more for serving

5 large eggs

2 cups whole milk

¼ teaspoon cayenne pepper

16 canned whole roasted peeled green chiles, halved lengthwise

2 cups grated Monterey Jack cheese

Corn tortillas, for serving

Sour cream, for serving

Sliced green onions, for serving

1. Preheat the oven to 325°F.

2. In a large skillet, combine the ground beef, onion powder, 1 tablespoon of the chili powder, 1 teaspoon of the salt, and the garlic.

4. And simmer for 10 minutes, stirring occasionally. Remove from the heat and let cool for 10 minutes.

6. The cayenne, remaining ½ teaspoon chili powder, and remaining ½ teaspoon salt . . .

3. Cook over medium-high heat until the meat is totally browned, stirring occasionally, about 7 minutes. Add the salsa and ½ cup water . . .

5. In a large pitcher or bowl, combine the eggs, milk . . .

7. And whisk until smooth.

8. In a large baking dish, layer half the green chiles, overlapping them as you go.

12. Meat . . .

16. Blacken the tortillas by holding them with tongs over the stovetop burner (or you can do this in a hot, dry cast-iron skillet).

9. Spoon half the meat mixture on top, making sure to get some of the juices in with it.

13. And cheese.

17. Cut the casserole into squares and serve with tortillas, salsa, sour cream, and a sprinkle of green onions.

10. Add half the Monterey Jack . . .

14. Pour the egg mixture on top and transfer to the oven.

THE ORIGINAL

To make the O.G. Lazy Chiles Rellenos casserole, simply omit the ground beef sauce (the first six ingredients). Assemble the chiles, cheese, and egg mixture as in the recipe, then bake for 45 minutes. Slice and serve with flour tortillas!

11. Then repeat the layers again, with chiles . . .

15. Bake until the eggs are completely set, about 50 minutes.

Uses canned green chiles!

TERRIFIC TEX-MEX

I would be remiss if I did not acknowledge how important Tex-Mex flavors are to the foods my family loves to eat. From the chiles to the colors to the spice, they show up in so much of what I cook. I think this category of food is probably at the top of my list of favorites (it's a very long list!), and I am so grateful it is in my life. While Tex-Mex ingredients and seasonings appear here and there throughout this cookbook, I wanted to compile a list of current faves the Drummond family is digging right now. Have your favorite bottle of hot sauce on hand. Things are about to get exciting (and easy) around here!

Best-of-Both-Worlds Enchiladas

MAKES 8 SERVINGS

When it comes to enchiladas, I can never decide between red and green . . . so I refuse to force myself to choose. This casserole not only unites two different sauce choices in one pan, it also gives you two different fillings (chicken or cheese) to choose from! Enchiladas are one of my huge weaknesses, and this one is just easy enough to pull together that it could be a little bit dangerous.

(Deliciously dangerous, that is. . . .)

16 corn tortillas (8 white corn and 8 yellow corn)

CHEESE FILLING

2 cups grated cheddar-Jack cheese

1 cup sour cream, at room temperature

½ cup pickled jalapeño slices, diced

2 green onions, thinly sliced

1 teaspoon Tex-Mex or taco seasoning

CHICKEN FILLING

1½ cups shredded cooked chicken (see page xxi)

Two 4-ounce cans chopped green chiles

2 tablespoons hot sauce (such as Cholula)

½ cup grated pepper Jack cheese

Pinch of kosher salt

½ teaspoon Tex-Mex or taco seasoning

ASSEMBLY

One 19-ounce can red enchilada sauce

One 19-ounce can green enchilada sauce

1 cup grated cheddar cheese

1 cup grated pepper Jack cheese

Sour cream, for serving

Hot sauce (such as Cholula), for serving

Cilantro leaves

1. Preheat the oven to 375°F.

2. Blacken the tortillas by holding them over the flame of your stove. (You can also put them in a dry cast-iron skillet over medium-high heat! Just takes a little longer.)

3. Make the cheese filling: In a medium bowl, combine the cheddar-Jack, sour cream, jalapeños, green onions, and Tex-Mex seasoning . . .

4. And stir until well mixed.

No cooking the filling or sauce ahead of time!

5. Make the chicken filling: In a medium bowl, combine the chicken, green chiles, hot sauce, pepper Jack, salt, and Tex-Mex seasoning . . .

6. And stir until well mixed.

7. To assemble: Spread ⅓ cup of the red enchilada sauce over one half of a large baking dish and ⅓ cup of the green enchilada sauce over the other half. Pour the rest of both enchilada sauces in separate pie plates for assembly.

8. Build the green enchiladas one by one by dunking one of the white corn tortillas in the green sauce . . .

9. Adding about 3 tablespoons of the chicken filling . . .

10. Rolling it up tight . . .

11. And placing it seam side down in the pan on top of the green sauce.

12. For the cheese enchiladas, dunk the yellow corn tortillas in the red sauce . . .

13. Add about 3 tablespoons of the cheese filling in a line down the center . . .

14. Roll it up tight . . .

15. And place it seam side down in the pan on top of the red sauce.

16. When the enchiladas are assembled, pour the rest of both sauces over their respective sides.

17. Top the red enchiladas with the cheddar and the green enchiladas with the pepper Jack.

18. Bake until the cheese is bubbling and barely starting to brown, 25 to 28 minutes. Let sit for 10 minutes.

19. Serve the enchiladas with sour cream, hot sauce, and cilantro. (One of each is plenty for a serving! I got a little ambitious with this plate . . . as I am wont to do.)

Mom and bride!

Chorizo and chiles give the burgers a kick!

Chorizo Burgers

MAKES 4 SERVINGS

It's hard to beat a good all-beef burger . . . but mixing in a little bit of chorizo sausage and green chiles might just edge out the original. These burgers are conversation pieces, piled high with bacon, lettuce, and tomato—and made even more amazing with a sunny-side up egg. It's plenty filling on its own, but a few doctored-up tots on the side never hurt anybody!

CILANTRO MAYO

¼ cup mayonnaise

¼ cup chopped fresh cilantro

Kosher salt and black pepper

BURGERS

1 pound ground chuck

½ pound fresh chorizo

One 4-ounce can diced green chiles, undrained

Kosher salt and black pepper

2 tablespoons olive oil

2 tablespoons salted butter

4 large eggs

4 burger buns, toasted

4 large lettuce leaves

1 large tomato, thinly sliced

8 slices thick-cut bacon, cooked to crisp and broken in half

Taco Tots (page 281)

1. Make the cilantro mayo: In a small bowl, stir together the mayonnaise, cilantro, and salt and pepper to taste.

2. Now it's time for the burgers! In a large bowl, combine the ground chuck, chorizo, green chiles, and a pinch each of salt and pepper . . .

3. And stir until well mixed.

4. Form the meat mixture into 4 patties a little wider than a burger bun. Heat a cast-iron skillet over medium heat and drizzle in the olive oil. Heat a separate nonstick skillet over medium-low heat and add the butter.

5. Put the patties in the cast-iron skillet and press them down slightly as they start cooking on the first side.

6. Crack the eggs into the nonstick skillet and sprinkle on salt and pepper to taste. Let the eggs continue to cook.

7. Back to the burgers! After they have cooked for about 5 minutes on the first side, flip them over and let them cook until completely cooked through, another 4 minutes.

8. Remove the eggs from the heat when the whites are set but the yolks are still soft. Set aside.

9. Time to build the burgers! For each burger, spread a generous amount of the cilantro mayo on both sides of the buns.

10. Set a burger on the bottom half of the bun, then pile the lettuce, tomatoes, and bacon on the top half.

11. Set a fried egg on top of the burger patty.

MAKE IT ITALIAN!

Speaking of adding sausage to burgers, I love this Italian version: Substitute Italian sausage for the chorizo, melt sliced mozzarella on the burger, and top with sliced roasted red peppers. Omit the egg and pile the burger with a mixture of arugula and basil. Drizzle with balsamic glaze and put on the top bun! Absolutely delicious.

12. Close the burger and serve with Taco Tots!

TACO TOTS

MAKES 4 (VERY GENEROUS!) SERVINGS

Cheesy, crispy tots with scrumptious taco flavor!

One 32-ounce bag frozen Tater Tots (about 5 cups)

1 tablespoon taco seasoning

1 cup grated Monterey Jack cheese

1. Preheat the oven to 450°F.

2. Pour the frozen tots onto a sheet pan. Sprinkle the taco seasoning on top . . .

3. And toss to coat. Bake until crisp, 28 to 30 minutes.

4. Pull the tots out of the oven, sprinkle them with the Monterey Jack . . .

5. And return to the oven to bake until the cheese is melted and starting to crisp in some places, about 5 minutes.

Fish Stick Tacos

MAKES 4 TO 6 SERVINGS

I first made these fish tacos during the early months of quarantine, and I fell in love with how incredibly easy they were to pull together. The "easy" comes in the form of frozen fish sticks—and not some crazy brand of elevated fish sticks from an upscale market. They're literally bulk fish sticks in a big plastic bag, and they probably cost pennies per stick! Add a bagged slaw, a quick avocado crema, and blackened tortillas and I promise you'll feel like you're in a restaurant in Newport Beach, grabbing a few fish tacos before you head back out to catch some gnarly waves wearing that cute green polka-dot bikini with the ruffles.

(I have a rich imagination.)

SLAW

One 14- or 16-ounce bag coleslaw mix

¼ cup chopped fresh cilantro

Juice of 2 limes

Kosher salt and black pepper

2 tablespoons olive oil

AVOCADO CREMA

1 cup store-bought guacamole

½ cup sour cream

¼ cup chopped fresh cilantro

Juice of 1 lime

Pinch of kosher salt

½ cup whole milk

TACOS

Twelve 4.5-inch flour tortillas

24 frozen fish sticks

½ cup chopped jarred pickled jalapeños

Hot sauce

Cilantro leaves

Lime wedges, for serving

1. First, make the slaw: In a medium bowl, combine the slaw mix, cilantro, lime juice, and salt and pepper to taste.

2. Add the olive oil . . .

3. And stir to combine. Set aside.

4. Make the avocado crema: In a small bowl, combine the guacamole, sour cream, cilantro, lime juice, and salt.

5. Pour in the milk . . .

6. And stir until smooth.

Made with bulk frozen fish sticks!

7. Make the tacos: Blacken the tortillas by holding them one by one over the stovetop burner (or you can put them in a dry cast-iron skillet over medium-high heat!). Set aside.

8. Bake the fish sticks according to the package directions.

9. To build the tacos, place 2 fish sticks on each tortilla.

10. Spoon on small piles of slaw . . .

11. And some chopped jalapeños . . .

12. Then a couple of dashes of hot sauce . . .

13. A good spoonful of avocado crema . . .

14. And cilantro leaves! Set a lime wedge on the side. (The lime gets squeezed on top before you dive in.)

Fish sticks, I love you!

FROZEN FISH STICKS = FABULOUS!

Fish tacos aren't the only inspired use for big, bulk bags of otherwise unremarkable fish sticks!

Fish Hoagie: Toast a hoagie roll, then slather the top and bottom with tartar sauce. Pile baked fish sticks onto the roll and top with cole slaw and pickles

Fish Stick Quesadillas: Sandwich several baked fish sticks with a generous amount of grated pepper Jack cheese between two flour tortillas. Grill them in a skillet with lots of butter.

Anchovy-Hater's Caesar Salad: Build your biggest, best Caesar and serve a few fish sticks on top or on the side. Boom!

Sheet Pan Quesadilla

MAKES ONE 13 × 18-INCH QUESADILLA (TO SERVE 9 TO 12)

I'm obsessed with quesadillas. However, in order to feed them to my not-small family, I have to either get several skillets going at once in order to have them all done at the same time or just cook the quesadillas in a single skillet one after another after another . . . for approximately three years.

Enter sheet pan quesadillas! I think these are pretty close to brilliant, and you get all the goodness of a cheesy chicken quesadilla without having to fry a single one! You'll fall in love with this method and will have fun coming up with your own combination of fillings to suit your fancy. (Note: This recipe is not fancy.)

½ cup (1 stick) salted butter, melted

Eight 10-inch flour tortillas

4 cups grated cheddar cheese

4 cups shredded cooked chicken (see page xxi)

2 teaspoons Tex-Mex or taco seasoning

One 6-ounce can diced green chiles, drained

½ cup sliced black olives

1 cup frozen fire-roasted corn, thawed

½ cup jarred salsa

4 cups grated Monterey Jack cheese

FOR SERVING

Hot sauce

Sour cream

Diced avocado

Lime wedges

Cilantro leaves

1. Preheat the oven to 450°F. Brush a sheet pan with one-third of the melted butter.

2. Arrange 1 tortilla at each end of the sheet pan and 2 tortillas on each long side, letting one-half of each tortilla hang over the side of the pan, and overlapping them as well.

3. Place 1 tortilla in the center so the whole bottom of the pan is covered.

4. Spread the cheddar all over the bottom, then sprinkle the chicken on top, getting both the cheese and the chicken out to the edges.

5. Sprinkle the Tex-Mex seasoning over the chicken . . .

6. Spoon the green chiles on top . . .

7. Evenly sprinkle on the black olives and roasted corn . . .

8. And add spoonfuls of salsa. This is getting interesting, isn't it?

9. Finally, sprinkle the Monterey Jack cheese in an even layer.

10. Place the last tortilla right in the center, pressing lightly.

11. Fold in the two tortillas on either side so that they overlap the tortilla in the center . . .

12. And fold in the other four tortillas so you have a neat tortilla rectangle!

13. Brush the rest of the melted butter all over the tortilla surface. You want the finished product to be buttery!

14. Place a second sheet pan on top, pressing gently to anchor. Carefully place the whole setup in the oven and bake the quesadilla for 20 to 22 minutes . . .

15. Until the tortillas are golden and the filling is bubbling and hot.

16. Cut the quesadilla into squares and serve with hot sauce, sour cream, avocado, lime wedges, and cilantro.

*No standing
at the skillet!*

Festive Pork Chops

MAKES 4 TO 8 SERVINGS

Oh, is this ever an amazing meal. And it's so very, very pretty! Golden pan-fried pork chops with a beautiful topping of two completely different salsas . . . it pretty much ticks all the boxes for me. (That it's served with gooey, cheesy rice on the side doesn't hurt either!)

EASY PINEAPPLE SALSA

1 cup diced fresh pineapple (or canned!)

½ red onion, finely diced

1 jalapeño, seeded and membranes mostly removed, finely diced

One 4-ounce jar diced pimientos

Juice of 2 limes

½ cup chopped fresh cilantro

CHOPS

1 cup all-purpose flour

2 teaspoons Tex-Mex or taco seasoning, plus more for sprinkling

1 teaspoon ground cumin

¼ teaspoon cayenne pepper

Kosher salt

8 boneless pork chops, medium thickness

½ cup vegetable oil

4 tablespoons (½ stick) salted butter

¼ cup tequila (optional)

2 cups good jarred salsa

FOR SERVING

Quick Mexican Rice (page 292)

Chopped fresh cilantro

1. Make the pineapple salsa: In a medium bowl, combine the pineapple, red onion, jalapeño, and pimientos.

4. Make the pork chops: In a shallow bowl, combine the flour, Tex-Mex seasoning, cumin, cayenne, and a pinch of salt . . .

2. Add the lime juice and cilantro . . .

5. And stir it with a fork until it's all mixed.

3. And stir to combine. Set aside.

6. Sprinkle the pork chops on both sides with Tex-Mex seasoning . . .

A 30-minute Tex-Mex meal!

7. Then dredge the chops in the seasoned flour . . .

8. Shaking off the excess. Keep dredging the pork chops, placing them on a plate as you coat them.

9. In a large nonstick skillet, heat the vegetable oil and butter over medium heat. Add the chops, working in batches as needed . . .

10. And cook them until deep golden brown on both sides, 2 to 3 minutes per side.

11. Remove them to a clean plate and cover with foil to keep warm.

12. Turn off the heat. Pour off all but 2 tablespoons of the fat, then pour in the tequila, if using. Stir into the warm pan.

Paige likes filming!

13. Turn the heat to medium and add the salsa.

14. Stir until the salsa is very hot, about 3 minutes.

15. Serve one or two chops with a generous spoonful of the salsa, then top with the pineapple salsa.

16. Serve with Quick Mexican Rice on the side and garnish with cilantro!

Middle-aged girls just wanna have fun!

QUICK MEXICAN RICE

MAKES 8 TO 10 SERVINGS

Mexican rice is one of my favorite sides, and this one comes together in pretty much 10 minutes . . . which is totally okay by me!

1 tablespoon olive oil

½ white onion, diced

1 garlic clove, pressed in a garlic press

1 teaspoon ground cumin

½ teaspoon cayenne pepper

¼ teaspoon ground turmeric

½ teaspoon kosher salt

½ teaspoon black pepper

One 15-ounce can tomato sauce

One 10-ounce can Ro*tel (diced tomatoes with green chilies)

Two 8.8-ounce bags microwavable white rice

1½ cups grated cheddar-Jack cheese

Minced fresh cilantro, for serving

2 green onions, sliced, for serving

1. In a deep skillet, heat the olive oil over medium-high heat. Add the onion, garlic, cumin, cayenne, turmeric, salt, and pepper . . .

2. And cook, stirring often, until the onion is soft and the spices are toasted, about 3 minutes.

3. Pour in the tomato sauce . . .

4. The Ro*tel . . .

5. And both bags of rice . . .

6. Stir together and cook, stirring often, until the rice is heated through and starting to absorb some of the sauce, about 5 minutes. Reduce the heat to low.

7. Cover the surface with the cheddar-Jack . . .

8. Then cover the pan and let the cheese melt completely, 2 to 3 minutes.

9. Sprinkle on the cilantro and green onions before serving.

Cheesy rice in minutes!

Honey-Chipotle Salmon

MAKES 4 SERVINGS

If you're looking for a lightning-fast meal with big flavor, it doesn't get any better than salmon—and adding a spicy-sticky chipotle glaze (spiked with tequila!) makes the whole thing just incomprehensibly tasty. And since the salmon is the star, you won't mind serving it with a side of microwave rice doctored up with cilantro and lime. Dinner will be done before you even know what hit you!

3 tablespoons olive oil

2 canned chipotle peppers in adobo sauce, finely chopped

2 tablespoons adobo sauce from the can

3 tablespoons honey

1 garlic clove, grated

2 green onions, thinly sliced

Grated zest and juice of 2 limes

¼ cup tequila (or chicken or veggie broth)

Kosher salt and black pepper

Four 6-ounce skinless salmon fillets

One 8.8-ounce bag microwavable white rice, for serving

¼ cup chopped fresh cilantro, plus cilantro leaves for garnish

1. In a small pitcher or bowl, combine 1 tablespoon of the olive oil, the chopped chipotle peppers, adobo sauce, honey, garlic, green onions, half the lime zest, half of the lime juice, the tequila, and salt and black pepper to taste . . .

2. And whisk until well combined.

3. Pat the salmon fillets dry with a paper towel, then season with salt and pepper.

4. Heat a large nonstick skillet over medium-high heat and cook the salmon for about 2 minutes on one side. Gently flip to the other side . . .

5. And pour in the glaze. Reduce the heat to medium-low . . .

6. And spoon the glaze over the salmon as it finishes cooking, about 4 more minutes.

Another 20-minute wonder!

7. Heat the rice in the microwave according to the package directions and dump it into a medium bowl.

9. And stir to mix!

11. And spoon extra glaze over the fish. (You can put the glaze on the rice, too!)

8. Add the remaining lime zest and lime juice, the chopped cilantro, and salt and pepper to taste . . .

10. Serve the salmon on a bed of cilantro-lime rice (I served mine with a little salad of grape tomatoes and cucumbers!) . . .

12. Garnish with cilantro leaves.

Cousins 4-Ever!

Tamale Pie

MAKES 8 TO 10 SERVINGS

Tamale pie is an incredibly hearty meal of flavorful/spicy meat with savory cornbread baked on top. It's a Tex-Mex classic, and also happens to be something my father-in-law, Chuck, has always loved. I like to add jalapeños to the cornbread for spice, of course . . . but also because it makes the topping look extra appealing. This serves football players and light eaters alike . . . just customize the size of the wedges you cut to suit the appetites!

2 tablespoons olive oil

1 medium onion, diced

2 garlic cloves, minced

2 pounds ground beef

One 19-ounce can red enchilada sauce

2 tablespoons Tex-Mex or taco seasoning

Kosher salt and black pepper

Two 8.5-ounce boxes corn muffin mix

1 cup buttermilk

2 large eggs

1 cup frozen fire-roasted corn, thawed

2 tablespoons salted butter, melted

1 cup grated cheddar cheese

1 cup grated Monterey Jack cheese

¼ cup jarred pickled jalapeño slices, drained

1. Preheat the oven to 400°F.

2. In a 12-inch ovenproof skillet, heat the olive oil over medium-high heat. Add the onion and garlic and cook, stirring often, until the onion starts to turn translucent, 3 to 4 minutes.

4. And cook until it's browned, about 5 minutes, breaking up the clumps as you go. Pour off the excess grease.

6. And stir to combine. Remove from the heat.

3. Add the ground beef . . .

5. Add the enchilada sauce, Tex-Mex seasoning, and salt and pepper to taste . . .

7. Pour the corn muffin mixes into a medium bowl.

8. Add the buttermilk, eggs . . .

10. Add the melted butter and stir until everything just comes together. Do not overmix!

12. Spoon the cornbread batter over the cheese and carefully spread it out.

9. And roasted corn and stir halfway to combine.

11. Sprinkle the grated cheeses over the meat mixture.

13. Arrange the jalapeño slices over the top and transfer to the oven.

The old floral cross . . .

14. Bake until the surface is deep gold and a toothpick inserted in the center comes out clean, 18 to 20 minutes.

15. Let sit for 10 minutes, then cut into wedges. It's messy and marvelous!

Corn muffin mix!

DESSERTS

Right here, in this chapter, is where everything is about to come full circle, to finally make perfect sense, and to send you away very, very happy. You are about to witness the unfolding of my current dessert life, and rather than tell you what you are going to see, I thought I'd lay out what you are not going to see: anything fussy. We don't have time for that! We need dessert now, and we need it to be easy, because who knows what tomorrow will bring? (This is exactly the kind of live-in-the-moment logic that got me in trouble in high school.)

Made with boxed cake mix!

Shortcut Tres Leches Cake

MAKES 15 SERVINGS

I'm getting ready to make a very strong statement. Are you ready? Here goes: *Tres leches cake is my favorite dessert on the planet.* I feel better just getting that off my chest! And it's absolutely true: To me, there is nothing more heavenly than this sweet, milk-soaked cake with a creamy topping. Absolutely nothing!

The original recipe calls for a from-scratch sponge cake which, while delicious, makes for a pretty long process. Enter: this super-easy cake mix version! The only downside is that tres leches cake can happen for me even more easily than before . . . and considering how sinful and indulgent this dessert is, I think I have a problem on my hands.

One 14-ounce can sweetened condensed milk

One 12-ounce can evaporated milk

¼ cup whole milk

½ teaspoon vanilla extract

One 16-ounce box white cake mix, baked in a 9 x 13-inch pan according to the package directions and cooled

One 15-ounce container frozen nondairy whipped topping (such as Cool Whip), thawed

One 12-ounce jar maraschino cherries, drained

½ cup rainbow sprinkles

1. In a large pitcher or spouted bowl, mix together the sweetened condensed milk, evaporated milk, whole milk, and vanilla.

3. Slowly pour the milk mixture over the surface, then give the cake time to soak up the liquid entirely, about 15 minutes.

5. Spread it all out into an even layer.

2. Use a toothpick to poke lots of holes all over the surface of the cooled cake.

4. Spoon the whipped topping all over the cake. (This is not an advertisement for Cool Whip. That said, I do keep them in business.)

6. Arrange the cherries in a grid (each slice of cake gets one!) and add a sprinkle of . . . well, sprinkles! Chill for 1 hour before serving if you have the time!

My favorite forever!

Rustic Strawberry Tart

MAKES 8 SERVINGS

This beautiful strawberry tart bakes for 30 minutes, but it takes only about 5 minutes to assemble before it goes in the oven. Refrigerated pie crust is the reason, and I like to double it up to make this tart big and beautiful. This is an impress-your-guests type of dessert . . . even if your guest is your sweetie. (Speaking of which: Mine loves this dessert!)

2 pints strawberries, hulled and halved

½ cup sugar

2 tablespoons all-purpose flour, plus more for dusting

1 teaspoon vanilla extract

1 teaspoon grated lemon zest

Juice of ½ lemon

2 refrigerated pie crusts, sold in rolls (such as Pillsbury)

Egg wash: 1 large egg whisked with 1 tablespoon water

⅓ cup apricot preserves

Sweetened whipped cream or whipped topping (such as Cool Whip), for serving

1. Preheat the oven to 400°F.

2. In a large bowl, combine the strawberries, sugar, flour, vanilla, lemon zest, and lemon juice . . .

3. And toss until well combined. Set aside while you prepare the crust.

4. On a lightly floured surface, unroll the pie crusts and overlap them so that half of one is over half of the other. Use a rolling pin to press them together and to roll them out to 11 x 19 inches.

5. Lay the crusts onto a sheet pan, letting the excess hang over the sides.

6. Arrange the strawberries in the center, taking care not to mound them too much . . .

7. Then fold up the edges of the dough to create a rim, pleating as you go.

Made with two store-bought pie crusts!

8. Use a pastry brush to lightly coat the rim with the egg wash.

9. Bake the tart for 30 minutes, rotating the pan halfway through so that it bakes and browns evenly. Let the tart sit for 15 minutes to allow the strawberries to set.

10. In a small saucepan, heat the apricot preserves with 2 tablespoons water over medium-low heat. Brush the strawberries with the melted preserves to give them a little extra gloss.

11. Slice and serve by itself or with whipped cream!

Visiting Paige at college!

Brownie S'mores Bars

MAKES 12 SERVINGS

Ahh, s'mores . . . how do I love thee? Let me count the ways.

This beautiful pan of brownies celebrates both everyone's favorite campfire dessert *and* the convenience beauty that is boxed brownie mix. In a dessert as crazy-busy as this one turns out to be, it almost seems a crime to waste time messing with fine chocolate and measuring dry ingredients. So steer clear of a life on the lam! These brownies will save you . . . in more ways than one.

Baking spray

One 18.4-ounce box brownie mix

¼ teaspoon kosher salt

Vegetable oil, as called for in the mix

Eggs, as called for in the mix

⅔ cup marshmallow creme

Three 1.55-ounce milk chocolate bars (such as Hershey's), 2 separated into segments and 1 chopped

1 sleeve (about 9 full-size) graham crackers, broken into pieces

One 10-ounce bag mini marshmallows

1. Preheat the oven to 350°F. Coat a 9 x 13-inch pan generously with baking spray.

2. In a large bowl, combine the brownie mix and salt, then add the vegetable oil, eggs, and water as directed on the package.

3. Stir the batter together and pour two-thirds of it into the pan, spreading it into an even layer.

4. Drop the marshmallow creme onto the batter in big dollops . . .

5. Then use a skewer or wooden toothpick to spread it around. (This isn't for a marbled appearance; just for spreading!)

6. Arrange the segments from the 2 chocolate bars evenly over the marshmallow creme layer . . .

7. Then sprinkle half of the graham cracker pieces on top . . .

8. And pour the rest of the brownie batter over the top. (It won't completely cover the graham crackers!)

12. Immediately stick the remaining bar of chopped chocolate and graham crackers into the surface. The chocolate will soften as it sits.

13. Sprinkle on any graham cracker crumbs that were left behind so that it's nice and messy! Let cool for a bit, then cut into squares. (Or you can skip the cooling and just dive right in!)

9. Bake until barely set in the center, about 30 minutes.

10. Pour the mini marshmallows over the top to completely cover the brownies and return to the oven.

11. Bake until the marshmallows are golden and soft, about 10 minutes. (Feel free to use the broiler if you'd like them a little darker!)

Duke, the water baby.

Boxed brownie mix saves time!

Easy as pie!

Root Beer Float Pie

MAKES 8 SERVINGS

Root beer floats are a taste from my childhood, and I have a confession to make: I never really liked them. Ha! Wasn't that a beautiful story?

Okay, to turn this tale around a little bit: While root beer floats aren't my favorite, this pie version is incredible! It uses both regular root beer and root beer extract to drive those flavors home, and it's a great make-ahead dessert for get-togethers or potlucks.

1 sleeve (about 9 full-size) graham crackers, crushed to fine crumbs

½ cup (1 stick) salted butter, melted

One 3.4-ounce package instant vanilla pudding mix

¼ cup cold whole milk

1 cup root beer, chilled

2 teaspoons root beer extract

One 8-ounce container frozen nondairy whipped topping (such as Cool Whip), thawed

Canned whipped cream

Maraschino cherries with stems, for garnish

1. Preheat the oven to 350°F.

2. In a large bowl, combine the graham cracker crumbs and melted butter . . .

4. Press the crumbs into a 9-inch pie plate and bake for 5 minutes. Let cool for 5 minutes.

6. Root beer, and root beer extract . . .

3. And stir until the crumbs are buttery and moist.

5. In a large bowl, combine the pudding mix, milk . . .

7. And whisk it until very smooth and thick, about 2 minutes.

8. Add the whipped topping . . .

10. Until completely combined.

12. Chill the pie for at least 2 hours for a softer pie or freeze it for an hour or more for a firmer pie.

9. And gently fold with a rubber spatula . . .

11. Pour the filling into the crust and spread it into an even layer.

(Note: The pie will deepen in color as it chills. Root beer magic!)

Them's my boys!

13. Add little dollops of canned whipped cream around the edge of the pie, then add cherries!

14. Slice and enjoy every bite!

Grilled Pineapple with Cream

MAKES 5 SERVINGS

I'm a huge fan of grilled fruit—especially pineapple, which always looks especially appealing after grilling. I serve this sweet dessert when I have big spreads of Tex-Mex food, but it's a great dessert for any old occasion. Today, for example!

This is an easy recipe to pull together, and you can use a couple of shortcuts to make it move even faster. It's a good one!

PINEAPPLE

½ large pineapple

Juice of 2 limes (grated the zest first and reserve for the whipped cream)

2 tablespoons coconut rum

1 tablespoon dark agave syrup or honey

Pinch of kosher salt

WHIPPED CREAM

1 cup heavy cream

1 tablespoon dark agave syrup or honey

Grated zest of 2 limes

FOR SERVING

1 tablespoon olive oil

Dark agave syrup or honey, for drizzling

Fresh mint leaves

1. Prepare the pineapple: Cut the top off the pineapple, then slice off the skin in sections.

3. Use a small round cutter to cut the core out of the centers (the cores can be discarded).

5. In a small pitcher or bowl, whisk the lime juice, coconut rum, agave syrup, and salt with a fork.

2. Cut 5 slices, then wrap the other half in plastic wrap and store it in the fridge for another use.

4. Place the slices in a dish and set it aside.

6. Pour the lime mixture over the pineapple and let it sit for 20 minutes, turning the pineapple over halfway through.

The perfect summertime treat!

7. While the pineapple is "marinating," make the whipped cream: In a medium bowl, combine the heavy cream, agave syrup, and lime zest . . .

8. And use a whisk (and all the energy you have left!) to whip it until soft peaks form. (You can also use a hand mixer; I won't judge you! Whipping cream by hand wears me slick.)

9. Preheat a grill pan over medium heat. Brush the grill with the olive oil, then grill the pineapple until nice grill marks have formed but the pineapple slices are still somewhat firm, 3 to 4 minutes per side.

10. Serve with big clouds of whipped cream on top, with a generous drizzle of agave syrup and a garnish of mint leaves.

Need a lift?

VARIATIONS

» *Take a shortcut by using thawed frozen nondairy whipped topping.*

» *Buy presliced pineapple (if your supermarket offers it) for another time-saver.*

» *Serve the pineapple with vanilla ice cream for an even more decadent dessert.*

Ice Cream Layer Cake

MAKES 8 TO 10 SERVINGS

When I made this on my Food Network show many, many moons (seven or eight years?) ago, it was a little bit of an afterthought! I needed to make an easy treat for that particular episode, and I grabbed a sad pound cake and assorted ice cream and just let it unfold as I went. This layered ice cream cake was the result and (as tends to happen when it isn't planned) the recipe wound up going viral—not in a TikTok way, but definitely in a 2013 Internet/social media way! I still love this cake when I don't feel like measuring, baking, or trying too hard. It's a winner!

One 10.75-ounce frozen pound cake (such as Sara Lee), thawed

2 generous scoops slightly softened vanilla ice cream

4 Reese's peanut butter cups, roughly chopped, plus more for sprinkling

2 generous scoops slightly softened chocolate ice cream

½ cup chocolate candies (such as M&M's), roughly chopped, plus more for sprinkling

2 generous scoops slightly softened coffee ice cream

½ bottle (about ⅓ cup) Magic Shell chocolate topping

2 tablespoons rainbow sprinkles

1. Remove the cake from its foil pan and cut it crosswise into 3 slices of equal thickness.

3. And use a spoon to spread the ice cream into an even layer.

5. Place the second layer of cake on top and press it firmly to pack it.

2. Lay an 18-inch piece of plastic wrap in the foil pan, allowing it to hang over the sides and lay one cake layer in the pan. Add the vanilla ice cream . . .

4. Sprinkle on the peanut butter cups.

6. Add the chocolate ice cream . . .

My old viral
ice cream cake!

7. And use a spoon to spread it out.

8. Sprinkle on the M&M's. (They add great color to the layers!)

9. Next comes the third layer of cake and the coffee ice cream!

10. Spread out the ice cream, then squeeze the Magic Shell all over the top. (Note: It isn't always lumpy like this! Mine got a little cold and I didn't have the patience to wait. Don't be like me.)

11. Immediately add the rainbow sprinkles. Sprinkle with more chopped peanut butter cups and M&M's.

12. Bring the four sides of plastic wrap over the cake, overlapping them . . .

13. Then freeze until you're ready to eat! (You can totally slice and serve immediately; it will just be a little bit soft.)

14. Keep it in the freezer, slicing as you need!

· ·

VARIATIONS

» *Make a tiramisu version by spooning 3 tablespoons sweetened coffee onto each layer of pound cake, and using only coffee ice cream.*

» *Change up the ice cream and candies however you'd like!*

Peach-Basil Shortcakes

MAKES 6 SERVINGS

Strawberry shortcake who? You need to get your hands on this marinated peach version! The biscuits are made with baking mix, the peaches come from the freezer, and the whole thing is just so lovely and tasty and wholesome. (Except for the booze. Sorry. Not sorry.)

This one's gonna win you over instantly!

SWEET BISCUITS

2½ cups baking mix
(such as Bisquick)

2 tablespoons granulated sugar

⅔ cup buttermilk

4 tablespoons (½ stick) butter,
melted

2 tablespoons turbinado (coarse)
sugar, for sprinkling

MARINATED PEACHES

3 cups frozen sliced peaches,
thawed

Grated zest of 3 oranges

⅓ cup granulated sugar

¼ cup orange liqueur
(or orange juice)

12 to 15 fresh basil leaves,
chiffonade-cut

FOR SERVING

Freshly whipped cream or
thawed whipped topping
(such as Cool Whip)

Fresh basil leaves

1. Preheat the oven to 375°F.

2. Make the sweet biscuits: In a large bowl, combine the baking mix and granulated sugar. Stir it to combine.

4. And keep mixing until combined. The dough will be clumpy!

6. Sprinkle the tops with the turbinado sugar and transfer to the oven.

3. Add the buttermilk and melted butter, using a fork to stir as you pour it in . . .

5. Divide the dough into 6 equal lumps (they should be craggy!) and place them in a well-seasoned cast-iron skillet or a 10-inch pie plate.

7. Bake until the tops are golden, 24 to 26 minutes. Set the biscuits aside to cool.

8. Marinate the peaches: In a large bowl, combine the peaches, orange zest, and granulated sugar.

9. Splash in the orange liqueur . . .

10. Then add the basil . . .

11. And toss to combine. Let the peaches marinate for 10 minutes at room temperature or up to 4 hours in the fridge.

12. To serve, split a biscuit in half through the middle and place a large billowy cloud of whipped cream on the bottom biscuit.

13. Spoon on several of the peaches, making sure to get some of the juices.

14. Top the peaches with a little more whipped cream . . .

15. Then lean the top of the biscuit against the bottom. Garnish with little basil leaves!

Best barn cat ever!

Baking mix + frozen peaches =
perfect peach shortcake!

The Best Chocolate Poke Cake

MAKES 8 TO 10 SERVINGS

The first time I ever had a poke cake, I was probably a preteen. I was at my grandmother Ga-Ga's house—which wasn't unusual since I think I was a bit of a handful—and she made a poke cake that called for chocolate instant pudding to be poured onto a yellow cake with holes. She and I shared a single warm piece, and to this day I'm not sure I've ever had a tastier cake.

This double-chocolate version is pretty darn close! I made it for a cowboy lunch when I'd been frying pork chops for what seemed like forever and I didn't have it in me to make dessert from scratch. They all declared the cake a success, which is just another reason cowboys are my favorite.

CAKE

One 16-ounce box chocolate cake mix, baked in a 9 x 13-baking pan according to the package directions

1 cup dark chocolate chips

One 14-ounce can sweetened condensed milk

½ cup whole milk

FROSTING

One 3.9-ounce package instant chocolate pudding mix

⅓ cup unsweetened cocoa powder

1¼ cups whole milk

One 8-ounce container frozen nondairy whipped topping (such as Cool Whip), thawed

1. Make the cake: Use the end of a wooden spoon or spatula to poke holes in the cake. Hence the name "poke cake!" (Sorry about the trypophobia trigger here.)

3. And the milk . . .

4. And stir until the mixture is combined; it'll be a milk chocolate color!

2. In a medium bowl, melt the chocolate chips in the microwave and stir until smooth. Pour in the sweetened condensed milk . . .

Chocolate overload!

5. Slowly pour the chocolate mixture over the cake, letting it get around the edges and inside the holes.

6. Let the cake sit for at least 10 minutes to soak up all the magic.

7. Make the frosting: In a medium bowl, combine the instant pudding mix, cocoa powder, and milk . . .

8. And whisk vigorously until very thick.

9. Add the whipped topping . . .

10. And use a rubber spatula to gently fold together until well combined.

11. Dump all the frosting on the cake . . .

12. And spread it into an even layer.

13. Cut into squares and serve immediately or cover and refrigerate the cake until you need it!

Coconut Cream Pie

MAKES 8 TO 12 SERVINGS

There are two big problems with this pie. The first problem is that I can't control myself around it. I know I say that about a lot of desserts, but it especially holds true with this one. It is so delicious, I can't see straight—and I can't keep it in my house if I ever have any left over after a get-together, because I'm powerless to resist it. The second problem is that it takes about 10 minutes to make, if that. And I guess that's a benefit, not a problem, if you need to make a super-fast dessert that's also amazingly tasty. But never mind—it's a problem. No question about it.

I'm glad we talked this through.

1½ cups very cold unsweetened coconut milk beverage (in the dairy section, such as Silk) or regular milk

Two 3.4-ounce boxes instant coconut cream pudding mix

One 8-ounce container frozen nondairy whipped topping (such as Cool Whip), thawed

1 store-bought 9-inch graham cracker pie crust

1 cup store-bought toasted coconut chips (from the snack aisle)

1. In a large bowl, combine the coconut milk and pudding mix . . .

3. Add half the container of whipped topping . . .

5. Pour the pudding mixture into the pie crust. (The lumps you see are little bits of coconut in the pudding. Oh my!)

2. And whisk gently for about 2 minutes while the mixture thickens. (It will turn beautifully golden, like a buried treasure!)

4. And use a rubber spatula to gently fold it in, as if it's a French confection.

6. Smooth it into an even layer and top it with the rest of the whipped topping.

7. Pile the toasted coconut in the center! You can eat the pie immediately, or you can chill it for a couple of hours. (Or both!)

VARIATIONS

» *Feel free to use a homemade graham cracker crust and/or freshly whipped cream if you'd like to add some from-scratch elements!*

» *Use this same formula with any flavor of instant pudding (butterscotch, chocolate, lemon, and so on) to change up your pie. Pick fun toppings as you wish!*

Sweet sisters!

Instant everything! Ready in 10 minutes.

Top-Secret Chocolate Cake

MAKES 10 TO 12 SERVINGS

As a middle-aged woman of the world, it is no secret to me that you can doctor up boxed cake mix to create a heavenly dessert. This trend took hold in the nineties, and it gave masses of people permission to forgo the measuring and mess of a from-scratch cake. But just in case your generation hid this eternal cake mix truth from you your whole life, I'm here to lift the veil. This is an incredibly simple way to ease into the cake-mix era in your life: a rich, very chocolaty cake that's such a cinch to make, it might become your go-to birthday cake request.

CAKE

Baking spray

1 cup whole milk

3 large eggs

One 15.2-ounce box dark chocolate cake mix (such as Duncan Hines)

1 tablespoon vanilla extract

½ cup (1 stick) salted butter, melted

1 cup semisweet chocolate chips

GANACHE AND TOPPING

½ cup heavy cream

⅔ cup semisweet chocolate chips

Assorted rainbow sprinkles

---

1. Preheat the oven to 350°F. Mist a 10-cup Bundt pan with baking spray.

2. Make the cake: In a bowl or large pitcher, whisk together the milk and eggs.

3. Add the cake mix and—this is important—feel no guilt or shame.

4. Stir until combined, then add the vanilla . . .

5. The melted butter . . .

6. And the chocolate chips . . .

The secret's out!
This cake is the best.

7. And stir again. Then pour the batter into the prepared pan. (Mine is spiky and fun, but a regular Bundt pan is perfect, too!)

8. Bake the cake until a toothpick inserted in the center comes out clean, about 40 minutes. Let the cake cool completely, then invert it onto a pretty plate or stand.

9. When the cake is cool, make the ganache: In a small saucepan, heat the cream over medium-low heat. Place the chocolate chips in a medium bowl and pour the hot cream over them. Let sit for 3 minutes . . .

10. Then stir vigorously for 1 to 2 minutes, until the ganache is smooth and glossy.

11. Slowly pour the ganache over the cooled cake, making sure to get it on the inside and outside. (Extra ganache can be refrigerated and reheated for another use!)

12. Before the ganache sets, add plenty of sprinkles!

13. Cut it into slices and dig in! You're in on the secret now!

ADD-INS AND ADD-ONS

- Add canned cherries, peanut butter, Nutella, chopped Andes mints, or M&M's to the cake batter before baking.

- Decorate with M&M's, chopped peanuts, white chocolate shavings, caramel sauce, or chopped toffee.

VARIATIONS

» *Top with crushed candy bars (such as Heath Bars, Snickers, and so on) instead of sprinkles.*

» *Substitute bittersweet chocolate chips for semisweet for a deep chocolaty flavor.*

» *Bake the cake in a 9 x 13-inch pan instead.*

Cinnamon Apples

MAKES 8 SERVINGS

Raise your hand if you remember these impossibly red cinnamon apples from Christmastimes of yore. (Raising both hands over here.) Well, big news! Cinnamon apples are still a thing, they *aren't* just for Christmastime, and they happen to be one of the easiest (and most fun) desserts in the world! The only catch is a several-hour chill time . . . but it's a small price to pay for one of the prettiest throwback treats in the world.

½ cup packed brown sugar

¾ cup cinnamon candies (such as Red Hots)

4 large Granny Smith apples, peeled, cored, and cut into eighths

4 tablespoons (½ stick) salted butter

One 16-ounce frozen pound cake (such as Sara Lee), cut into 8 slices

Vanilla ice cream, for serving

Mint leaves, for garnish

1. In a large saucepan, combine the brown sugar and 2½ cups water and stir over medium-high heat until dissolved.

3. And cook, stirring, until the candies have fully melted and the liquid is bubbling, about 10 minutes.

5. Remove the apples to a heatproof medium bowl. Boil the syrup for about 5 minutes, until slightly thickened . . .

2. Add the cinnamon candies . . .

4. Add the apples, bring to a boil, and cook until the apples are tender but not mushy, about 5 minutes.

6. Then pour the syrup over the apples. Make sure the apples are totally submerged, then cover the bowl with plastic wrap and refrigerate for 4 hours.

7. This is what happens in the fridge! So fun and so very, very red.

9. Serve a piece (or two) of cake with a little (or a lot of!) vanilla ice cream . . .

11. Garnish with mint leaves.

8. To serve, melt the butter on a griddle over medium heat and toast the pound cake, about 3 minutes per side.

10. And a big, beautiful helping of apples and syrup!

VARIATION

» *For a simpler presentation, just serve dishes of apples with a little whipped cream on top!*

A man and his truck.

Just like your
great-grandma
used to make!

Easy "Fried" Ice Cream

MAKES 4 SERVINGS

Fried ice cream is an incredibly decadent dessert, but through much trial and error (emphasis on error), I've found it pretty difficult to make at home with any consistency. I adore this recipe as a much-easier version of fried ice cream. It causes far fewer tears with all the incredible flavor! While it isn't a permanent stand-in for the original dessert, it sure will tide you over between trips to that one restaurant in your town that still serves it.

(Do any restaurants still serve fried ice cream? I haven't seen it in a million years!)

2 tablespoons salted butter

1 cup cornflakes, crushed

1 tablespoon sugar

⅛ teaspoon ground cinnamon

Pinch of kosher salt

4 scoops ice cream

Canned whipped cream, for serving

1 tablespoon rainbow sprinkles, for serving

4 maraschino cherries with stems, for serving

1. In a nonstick skillet, melt the butter over medium heat. Add the crushed cornflakes . . .

2. And toast, stirring occasionally, until golden, about 5 minutes. Watch them so they don't burn!

3. Turn off the heat. Add the sugar, cinnamon, and salt . . .

4. And stir to coat the cornflakes in the seasoning . . .

5. Then pour them out onto a plate to cool completely.

6. To serve, use a spoon to sprinkle (and press) the crumbs onto a scoop of ice cream.

7. Top with whipped cream, sprinkles, and a cherry!

Fried ice cream without the tears!

Frozen pound cake saves tons of time!

Blackberry Icebox Cake

MAKES 8 SERVINGS

This cake makes me happy! I first made it during the early months of quarantine, and it was pulled together using fresh and frozen staples I had on hand. The headline is that it uses a frozen pound cake as its foundation—such a time-saver—and because of the whipped cream-fruity goodness, it's hard to tell the cake wasn't made from scratch. You can throw it together right before serving, or—if you have the time—you can pop it in the fridge and let it develop that wonderfully soft icebox cake vibe.

Now go make this cake! I promise it'll make you happy, too.

One 16-ounce frozen pound cake (such as Sara Lee), thawed

1 tablespoon salted butter

1½ cups heavy cream

2 tablespoons powdered sugar

1½ cups fresh blackberries, halved, plus whole blackberries for garnish

5 tablespoons blackberry jam

Grated zest of 1 lemon, plus more zest for garnish

Juice of ½ lemon

Fresh mint leaves, for garnish

1. Using a serrated knife, shave off the very top crust of the pound cake.

2. Crumble the crust into fine crumbs using your fingers (or you can use a fine grater).

3. In a small skillet, melt the butter over medium-low heat. Add the crumbs . . .

4. And toast the crumbs, shaking the pan and occasionally stirring them, until deep golden brown, about 5 minutes. Watch them carefully! Turn off the heat and let them cool.

5. Slice the cake crosswise into 3 equal pieces.

6. In a medium bowl, use a mixer to beat the cream and powdered sugar to stiff peaks.

7. In a separate bowl, combine the halved blackberries, blackberry jam, lemon zest, and lemon juice . . .

8. And stir to mix everything together.

9. Lay an 18-inch-long piece of plastic wrap in the pound cake's foil pan so that it hangs over the sides. Press one cake layer in the pan . . .

10. Then spread one-third of the blackberry mixture on top . . .

11. And one-third of the whipped cream.

12. Place a second cake layer on top, pressing lightly to remove any air pockets.

The middles!

13. Continue building the next two layers, ending with the last of the whipped cream. Fold the plastic wrap over the top and refrigerate the cake for up to 12 hours. (You may skip this step if you want to serve the cake immediately.)

14. When you're ready to serve the cake, use the plastic wrap overhangs to lift it out of the pan.

15. Place it on a platter or cake stand and even out the top with the back of the spoon.

16. Sprinkle on the cake crumbs . . .

17. Then garnish with the whole blackberries, mint leaves, and lemon zest.

· ·

VARIATIONS

» *To save a step, use frozen nondairy whipped topping (such as Cool Whip) instead of freshly whipped cream.*

» *Substitute strawberries and strawberry preserves for the blackberries and blackberry jam.*

» *Blueberries would be lovely, too! (So would raspberries!)*

» *Make a tiramisu version by brushing each layer of cake with sweetened espresso, mixing mascarpone with the whipped cream, and adding lots of shaved chocolate. Divine!*

18. Slice it and brag that this beautiful dessert came together using a frozen pound cake.

(Actually, scratch that. You don't have to tell anyone!)

The Best Potluck Dessert Ever

MAKES 12 SERVINGS

This is an old-time potluck dessert that has made the rounds in small-town churches everywhere, and it is a food snob's worst nightmare. When you see the ingredient list, you'll quickly understand why. That said, there is something strangely delicious about this sweet, and it's always the first dish to be empty on the dessert table!

Cooking spray

1 rounded cup all-purpose flour

1½ cups finely chopped pecans

½ cup (1 stick) salted butter, melted

One 8-ounce package cream cheese, at room temperature

1 cup powdered sugar

1 teaspoon vanilla extract

Two 8-ounce containers frozen nondairy whipped topping (such as Cool Whip), thawed

One 5.1-ounce package vanilla instant pudding mix

One 5.9-ounce package chocolate instant pudding mix

3 cups whole milk

1 cup mini chocolate chips

1. Preheat the oven to 350°F. Mist a 9 x 13-inch baking dish with cooking spray.

2. Add the flour, 1 cup of the pecans, and the melted butter to the dish . . .

4. Then press it into the pan to form an even layer.

6. In a medium bowl, combine the cream cheese, powdered sugar, and vanilla . . .

3. And stir until it comes together . . .

5. Bake until the edges are golden, about 20 minutes. Set aside to cool completely.

7. And use an electric mixer to beat it until fluffy, scraping the bowl halfway through.

Made by church ladies everywhere!

8. Add 1 container of the whipped topping and fold it in gently.

9. In a separate medium bowl, combine the vanilla and chocolate pudding mixes and the milk . . .

10. And whisk until it thickens, about 1 minute.

11. Spread the cream cheese mixture in an even layer on the cooled crust . . .

12. Then spread the chocolate mixture on top.

13. End with the second container of whipped topping! This cake is naughty, man!

14. Decorate the top with the mini chocolate chips and the remaining ½ cup pecans. Serve it immediately for a softer dessert or chill it for up to 12 hours for a firmer dessert.

Enjoy every single bite!

Mug Cakes

EACH RECIPE MAKES A SINGLE-SERVING MUG CAKE

There's nothing more magical than a mug cake! They're easy, quick, and exceedingly customizable. If there's a cake on this beautiful earth that you love, it can be made into a mug cake. Here are three of my go-to flavors! Each one is mixed right in the mug, and each one takes 90 seconds to "bake"! Cake has never, ever been so easy.

CHOCOLATE CARAMEL MUG CAKE

A rich chocolate mug cake with chewy bits of caramel and a little crunch of pecan. It's like a turtle candy in mug cake form!

3 tablespoons all-purpose flour

3 tablespoons sugar

2 tablespoons unsweetened cocoa powder

¼ teaspoon baking powder

Pinch of kosher salt

3 tablespoons whole milk

3 tablespoons vegetable oil

Splash of vanilla extract

2 individually wrapped soft caramel squares, cut in half

1 tablespoon semisweet chocolate chips

1 tablespoon finely chopped pecans

1 heaping tablespoon marshmallow creme or vanilla ice cream, for topping

Caramel sauce, for topping

1. In a 12-ounce microwave-safe mug, combine the flour, sugar, cocoa powder, baking powder, and salt. Stir to combine.

2. Add the milk, vegetable oil, and vanilla . . .

3. And stir with a fork until the batter is all mixed.

4. Add the caramel pieces, chocolate chips, and pecans . . .

5. And stir to incorporate.

6. Run a damp paper towel around the inside of the mug to clean it . . .

7. Then microwave for 90 seconds! The cake will puff up pretty high in the microwave and immediately start to settle when you pull it out. (Be careful—some mugs get hot!)

8. Top the mug cake with marshmallow creme . . .

9. And caramel sauce! Let it sit for a minute or two before eating, as the filling can be hot.

"Don't hate me because I'm beautiful."

Chocolate Caramel

Gingerbread

Confetti

Cake in 90 seconds!

CONFETTI MUG CAKE

The cutest, happiest mug cake in the world! This is perfect for an impromptu birthday treat, or anytime your day needs a few sprinkles to set it back on track.

¼ cup all-purpose flour

3 tablespoons sugar

½ teaspoon baking powder

3 tablespoons whole milk

2 tablespoons vegetable oil

1 tablespoon clear vanilla extract (regular vanilla is fine, too!)

1 tablespoon rainbow sprinkles, plus more for topping

Canned whipped cream, for topping

Sliced strawberries, for topping

2. And stir with a fork until mixed. Wipe the inside clean with a damp paper towel.

4. And use the fork to just press them lightly into the batter (no need to stir!).

1. In a 12-ounce microwave-safe mug, combine the flour, sugar, baking powder, milk, vegetable oil, and vanilla . . .

3. Add the sprinkles . . .

5. Microwave the mug cake for 90 seconds! Carefully remove the mug . . .

6. And top with whipped cream and sliced strawberries. Let it sit for 2 minutes before eating.

GINGERBREAD MUG CAKE

Brown sugar, spice, and everything nice. That's what this mug cake is made of!

¼ cup whole milk

3 tablespoons vegetable oil

1 heaping tablespoon molasses

¼ cup plus 2 tablespoons all-purpose flour

3 tablespoons packed brown sugar

½ teaspoon baking powder

½ teaspoon pumpkin pie spice

Pinch of kosher salt

Canned whipped cream, for topping

Caramel sauce, for topping

1. In a 12-ounce microwave-safe mug, combine the milk, vegetable oil, and molasses.

4. Microwave the mug cake for 90 seconds. Carefully remove the mug . . .

5. And top with whipped cream and caramel sauce. Let it sit for 2 minutes before eating.

2. Add the flour, brown sugar, baking powder, pumpkin pie spice, and salt . . .

3. And mix well. Use a damp paper towel to wipe the inside clean.

ACKNOWLEDGMENTS

To my amazing editor, Cassie Jones Morgan. We did our first cookbook together over twelve years ago and working with you is still a complete joy! Thank you for being the very best.

To my agent, Susanna Einstein, and the team at William Morrow: Jill Zimmerman, Anwesha Basu, Liate Stehlik, Tavia Kowalchuk, Ben Steinberg, Rachel Meyers, Pam Barricklow, Lucy Albanese, Mumtaz Mustafa, and Anna Brower, for your awesome support through the years (and especially through the past year!).

To Kris Tobiassen, for laying out and arranging and designing and perfecting. Thank you for making this cookbook look fabulous!

To Ed Anderson, for taking all the food photos so that I could focus on the cooking. Thank you for spending time in Oklahoma and sharing your talents.

To my amazing right-hand fella, Trey Wilson, and to Tiffany Taylor, Matt Taylor, Allison Jordan, and Seth Jordan, my beyond-incredible cookbook team! Man, was this a marathon—you're all freaking fantastic!

To Haley Carter, for your awesome support over the past many, many years! I couldn't do it without you.

To my sweet, wonderful friends—childhood, high school, college, and beyond. You know who you are, and you know how much you mean to me.

To my parents, in-laws, and siblings. I love you so much.

To Alex, Mauricio, Paige, Stuart, Bryce, Jamar, and Todd—all my children (well, and nephew and son-in-law!) What a crazy couple of years it's been. I love you guys!

To Ladd, for being handsome. (Oh, and for your love and support . . . and for basically everything. I love you.)

To all of you, for supporting me and letting me continue to share recipes and stories with you. I keep you all in mind, whether I'm filming my cooking show or writing recipes—and I can't thank you enough for keeping me motivated and inspired!

UNIVERSAL CONVERSION CHART

OVEN TEMPERATURE EQUIVALENTS	MEASUREMENT EQUIVALENTS *Measurements should always be level unless directed otherwise.*
250°F = 120°C	⅛ teaspoon = 0.5 mL
275°F = 135°C	¼ teaspoon = 1 mL
300°F = 150°C	½ teaspoon = 2 mL
325°F = 160°C	1 teaspoon = 5 mL
350°F = 180°C	1 tablespoon = 3 teaspoons = ½ fluid ounce = 15 mL
375°F = 190°C	2 tablespoons = ⅛ cup = 1 fluid ounce = 30 mL
400°F = 200°C	4 tablespoons = ¼ cup = 2 fluid ounces = 60 mL
425°F = 220°C	5⅓ tablespoons = ⅓ cup = 3 fluid ounces = 80 mL
450°F = 230°C	8 tablespoons = ½ cup = 4 fluid ounces = 120 mL
475°F = 240°C	10⅔ tablespoons = ⅔ cup = 5 fluid ounces = 160 mL
500°F = 260°C	12 tablespoons = ¾ cup = 6 fluid ounces = 180 mL
	16 tablespoons = 1 cup = 8 fluid ounces = 240 mL

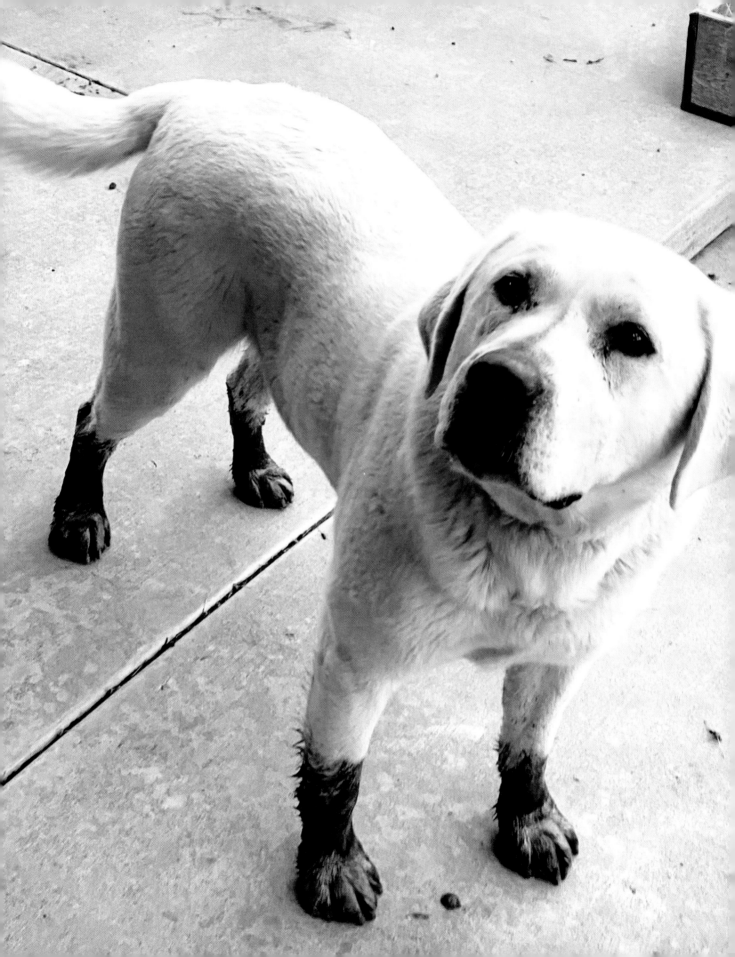

INDEX

The End